MENTAL HEALTH

A collection of poetry, short prose, interviews and personal stories from around the world on the themes of mental health.

Compiled by Robin Barratt

MENTAL HEALTH

ISBN: 9798860545991
© Robin Barratt and all the authors herein, September, 2023

Published independently by Robin Barratt
www.RobinBarratt.co.uk

Illustrations by Daniella Barratt

TRIGGER WARNING!

This book contains poetry, personal stories, short prose and interviews about addiction, trauma, personality disorders, suicidal thoughts, self-harming, depression and other significant mental health issues.

INTRODUCTION

"Having had a number of mental health challenges throughout my life, compounded by trauma and a difficult childhood, I have always found books and words and poetry both therapeutic and cathartic, and a really good catalyst for coping when things become particularly difficult. And so I founded POETRY FOR MENTAL HEALTH, aimed at motivating and inspiring other people with mental health challenges to put pen to paper and transform their thoughts, feelings, emotions and experiences into words.

"No matter what your age, background and experience, culture or identity; whether an established writer and poet with many published titles to your credit, or an aspiring poet who has never written a word of poetry in your life, my philosophy at Poetry for Mental Health is to embrace, welcome and support everyone, everywhere suffering from mental health challenges, and help you cope through words and poetry. Get writing!"

ROBIN BARRATT
Founder: POETRY FOR MENTAL HEALTH
www.poetryformentalhealth.org

NOTE:

For a small number contributors to this anthology, English is not their first language and, unlike other poetry platforms, I don't heavily edit a poet's own work (if I did, it would then not be their own work!), so please focus on a poet's messages and meanings, and not necessarily on any grammatical mistakes or translated imperfections.

ALSO BY POETRY FOR MENTAL HEALTH

ADDICTION
A collection of poetry, short prose, and personal stories from around the world on the theme of addiction.
Published June, 2023
ISBN: 9798396831698
181 pages, 69 contributors.

SUICIDE Vol.2
A collection of poetry, short prose, interviews and personal stories from around the world on the themes of suicide and self-harm.
Published April, 2023
ISBN: 9798388770455
275 pages, 89 contributors, 29 countries.

SUICIDE
A collection of poetry and short prose from writers around the world on the themes of suicide and self-harm.
First published 2019, Updated December 2022
ISBN: 9781091029347
175 pages, 48 contributors, 20 countries.

CONTENTS

"Mental health is a state of mental well-being that enables people to cope with the stresses of life, realize their abilities, learn well and work well, and contribute to their community."
World Health Organisation.

"Mental health refers to our emotional, psychological, and social well-being. We all have mental health. Our mental health affects how we think, feel, and act. It also impacts on how we cope, interact and form relationships with others, as well as our daily functioning."
NHS.org

MENTAL HEALTH

A collection of poetry, short prose, interviews and personal stories from around the world on the themes of mental health.

Kathy Sherban's story

How do I share a story that makes absolutely no sense to me? Truth be told, I will never understand how my life turned sideways at such a young age and continued to spin for years to follow. So ... here I am, 58 years old, spending my 'golden years' at our cottage by the lake, where the air is clear, nights are crisp; yet my chest feels heavy and I struggle to breathe. Most days the sun shines brightly warming everything around me, but inside I feel cold. I watch as children run along the beach raucously laughing while playing with their friends yet I can barely crack a smile. This is what depression looks like from my lens. I walk through life in a perpetual state of melancholy, rarely leaving that space regardless of the circumstance, joy my ever-elusive unicorn.

Imagine, if you will, that you are a child from a less than modest lifestyle, your world a shaky platform, instability a close friend, a family in constant turmoil, all worn like a pair of comfortable old shoes. Ignorant to what is considered normal; I was completely unaware that my fragile universe was about to collapse cutting me loose from family ties, leaving me adrift in a sea of turmoil for years to come. At nine years old my trajectory was forever altered by the sins of my father and the deeds of my mother. One inconceivable action by my father, that took only minutes to commit, robbed my childhood, stole my courage, self-esteem, trust and faith in humankind. It has reverberated through my soul and skipped like a scratched record through every year of my life. After being stripped of my dignity and self-respect, my entire sense of value was erased and replaced with self-loathing, anger and confusion. Everyone asked "what's wrong with her?", rather than "what happened to her?" ... and so, the saga began ... and continues until this day.

To the best of my recollection (memories do vary from the perspective of others) my story began like many other under privileged families; my parents were both uneducated, struggling to survive with very little support from their families. Mom was your typical stay at home wife, Dad, on the other hand, lived a life of ill repute; never having done an honest day's work (nor did he ever intend to) the law eventually came calling for him. When I was about five years old, Dad went to prison for carrying a concealed weapon - essentially leaving our family destitute. As a side note I discovered after he passed away in 2014, that he was a safe cracker. I suspect (but can't confirm) that he was also charged with theft at the time of his arrest. Unable to support our family, the Children's Aid Society (Child Welfare Services) stepped in to take temporary custody of my two brothers and I until Mom sorted herself out. During Dad's incarceration, Mom petitioned him for divorce and moved on with another man named Terry. He was handsome, kind, and a breath of fresh air. Where my father was absent and angry, Terry was warm and fully engaged. Eventually Terry proposed to Mom, and they became engaged to be married until my strict Roman Catholic (maternal) grandparents got wind of it. Grandma and Grandpa refused to acknowledge Mom's divorce, nor did they sanction her marrying Terry, who was a Protestant no less! That was the end of our almost happily ever after. Long story short, Terry disappeared from our lives and simultaneously Dad was released from prison returning to reclaim his wife and family.

I have no memory of my dad prior to him going to jail, however, my recollection of him post prison have left emotional scars that probably will never heal. Life became akin to walking through a minefield, never knowing what would set off my father's anger, his rage knew no boundaries. Children were meant to be seen not heard, discussion was not encouraged, rules were established and expected to be obeyed without exception. Punishment ranged from being banished to our bedroom (there was only one in the entire house!) to dad taking his belt off and laying a whooping our bare bottoms. Mom didn't provide shelter or respite from Dad's outbursts; in fact, she became (and still is to this day) an ostrich with her head in the sand ignoring everything that was unravelling around her. We, the children, were left defenseless with the exception of my maternal grandmother, who seemed to be the only person who would stand up to my father. As I got older, the battles between myself and my parents raged on, escalating to where one day my dad told me to pack my suitcase (didn't know I owned one?) and get out of his house. At fifteen years old, Mom dropped me off on the main street of our tiny little town, with my shabby brown suitcase in tow, Bryan Adams playing on the radio, leaving me alone to fend for myself.

These memories haunt me; my feelings of abandonment and isolation continue to weigh heavily on my shoulders; joy and happiness elude me. Although my survival instinct kicked in and has remained a steadfast companion throughout my life, no measure of success has ever replaced the emptiness I have felt as a result of my childhood trauma. Truth be told, I am only just beginning to acknowledge and accept my story as a success to be celebrated, not in spite of, but because of where my journey has taken me.

Today, I am sadly estranged from the majority of my family with very few exceptions, I can count my true friends on one hand, there are many acquaintances in my life, but they don't really count for much. This is my truth; relationships are quite difficult for me to maintain as a result of my deep-rooted trust issues stemming back to my unfortunate beginnings. On a more positive note, I am happily married to a wonderfully kind, patient and loving man who has walked many miles of this journey with me. My son and I have a very close relationship - although I know the strain of my fractured familial ties weighs heavily on him. I try very hard to be a glass half-full person; choosing to remain optimistic that tomorrow will be brighter regardless of how dark I find today.

Social media allows me to 'appear' normal, to blend with everyone else without distraction. People enjoy reading my poetry, love seeing my pictures from various exotic locations around the world, transporting themselves into my adventures. They see 'happiness'; they don't see the truth, which is far less interesting, much less glamorous, and definitely not enviable. I struggle daily with depression and PTSD - admittedly some days are better than others. I have learned over the years that I require a purpose to get up, show up, and live my best life each day. Accepting a part-time job has helped motivate me to engage in my own life, akin to breathing fresh air into a stale room. Working has given me something other than my own issues to focus on, mental stimulation to fan the flames of my brain, nourishment for my writing, physical energy. I remain a work in progress, relying heavily on my tight inner circle, keeping my trusted therapist on speed dial to ensure I don't slide down my slippery slope of depression. As I share my truth one story at a time, my goal is to shed light on my mental wellness journey as a way to connect with others, ultimately unveiling the truth behind our struggles.

Poetry by Kathy Sherban

CHOICES

She ...
chooses "XY" over "X" squared
Her ...
husband, brother, sons, friends
She ...
buries her head deep in the sand
Her ...
eyes conceal guilt, ears tune out truth
She ...
excuses their behavior while condemning mine
I ...
was left bleeding, cut to the core
My ...
trajectory altered; world turned upside down
I ...
was left hurt n' abandoned
We ...
were irreparably fractured, two hearts broken
A ...
mother n' daughter
the unforgiving tragedy of misplaced allegiance
Our ...
family fatale
forever altered by the sins of thy father n' deeds of thy mother

THE HAUNTING

Haunting memories
years gone past
breaking my spirit
a soul harassed

Emotional scars
a harsh decree
house of horrors
I paid the fee

Each event
a blinding trigger

flashbacks holler
hello gravedigger

Nightmares persist
rise from the dust
a demons embrace
forbidden lust

Exorcist needed
kill the ghost
give me peace
find a new host

Originally published in my book *Accidental Poetess* (FriesenPress).

TRAUMA

The shattering event(s) that create your mold ...
That set the stage for your future to unfold ...
The story of carnage yet to be told ...
The sadly ever after for others to behold ...

Originally published in my book *Accidental Poetess* (FriesenPress).

REFLECTION

Have you never, ever
hidden your shame
worn a scarlet letter
assumed all the blame
thirsted for love
honor's thy name
flirted with danger
in a zero-sum game

Have you never, ever
shook things up
tested the limits
filled up your cup
drank a little poison
thirsted for blood
spewed some vulgarities
threw a handful of mud

Have you never, ever
basked in the glow
longed for the sunshine
gone with the flow
chased your dreams
reached for the sky
discovered utopia
learned how to fly

Have you never, ever
fully exhaled
shed your armour
inner beauty unveiled
spawned forgiveness
hope entertained
buoyed in triumph
whilst victory proclaimed

ABOUT KATHY
Kathy resides in Ontario, Canada. She is a writer, poet and author of *Accidental Poetess, Poetic PicaZZo's, Brain Babel: A Poet's NoiZe* and *That's Amore*. Her work has also been published in numerous global anthologies and international literary magazines.
W: www.kathysherban.ca
FB: @Kat's Poetry Korner
FB: @kats_kradle
Instagram: @kat_s_kradle
X: @kathysherban

Poetry by Donna McCabe

WHEN THE BLUES COME CALLING ...

Feeling enclosed
Alone
Strange thoughts keep
Messing with my head
Drawing my soul
Into a pit of despair
Strength of body
Will and mind
Are numb
A connection laid bare
Eyes fixed upon nothing
Staring into space
Unable to rejoice in anything.

INKED FRUSTRATIONS

Tears of a poets fall
Droplets of sorrow and pain
Finding their way onto paper
Where in ink they flow again
Words of deep emotions
That have so long been repressed
Now ready to see the light of day
Ready to be expressed.

HEALING...

Blinded by fear
But you helped me see
Drowning in sorrow
But you helped me swim
Numbed to emotion
But you helped thaw my feelings
Turned a blackened and bruised shell
Into a fresh beating soul
Through your timeless patience and love
Your healing hands and heart
Gave back a life to treasure.

MY MIND...

A staircase to the stars
Unlocking so many dreams and realities
Storing all life memories of many
Making the unreal a possibility
Concepts come to life
A powerful tool when lit up with light
A dark place to be at times too.

AMELIORATING

Laying here
Lost in nature
In scents and sounds divine
Resting awhile
Absorbing the energy in
Feeling it uplift and heal
Restore and renew
In ways only mother nature can do

SURVIVOR

All those times
When I have been crippled
Emotionally and physically
When darkness has descended
In violent and turbulent storms
And I had to fight single handedly
To overcome them all
Was written in my destiny

ABOUT THE POEMS
"These poems were written as a way of dealing with difficult and dark periods of my life, some of which I'm still dealing with to this day. I lost my dad to suicide at 15, and still have many other difficult hurdles to content with, as well as trying to process what he'd done too - it still has major impacts to this very day, as well as managing my own health issues of epilepsy and mental health. I also lost my 23 year-old son in June, and am currently having to deal the shock and grief and on-going investigation of his passing - he also suffered from seizures but was never diagnosed with epilepsy, and had a lot of mental health issues in his life too. I do believe personally that the

therapy of writing has brought me much joy and healing over the
years, and helped soothe a lot of the pain."

ABOUT DONNA
Donna is a poet with over twenty years of experience, whose variety of work has gained her multiple accolades over the years within her field of literature. She has been published both nationally and internationally in journals, magazines and anthologies, and is a highly respected admin in multiple social media groups. She has recent collaborations with Ala Ilescu, an up-and-coming Canadian artist, resulting in a beautiful book of poetry and artwork entitled *Explosion Of Love*.
FB: @Poemsbydonnamccabe
Instagram: @donnamccabe_

Poetry by Ella Pedersen-Jones

SHATTERED VASE

My heart is beating in someone else's blood.
It couldn't be mine.
I have never belonged to this body.
I am just taking up the empty space, is all.

It really hurts to know that I won't have control.
When it creeps up on both you and me.
It rings out like a bullet aimed at the wrong target.
I'm afraid to speak, because I shiver at the thought.
What if it isn't really me that's staring you right in the eye?

I breakdown at the slightest change in tone.
I become something so vicious and so full of fright.
But deep inside is the real me.
Clawing on the walls and begging for some light.

That smashing of the glass is just a cover.
When I'm down on my knees,
bleeding over and over, just picking up the invisible pieces.
Shifting between a whimper and a laugh.
It just hurts so bad to cry,
but hurts so much more to smile while facing the closing door.

I plead within myself but what's the use?
I don't want to wake up, but I don't want to die.
Just having to use my mind is like an override.
Cause who really lives happily while they are alive.

I want to change even more than you want me to, you know?
And while the wounds are still fresh, could you sow them up?
I feel I should leave.
You wouldn't suffer as much if I weren't here.

I treat you like crap because I don't know what else to do.
I blame my pitiful existence on my crumbling mental health.
I turn into a broken clock.
Staying in the same place, never changing as life moves forward.
But this time, it's just without me.
And maybe that's how it should be.

ABOUT THE POEM
"This poem is a reference to my recent struggles with Borderline Personality Disorder. It describes the feeling of not belonging in your own body, as well as feeling monstrous."

ABOUT ELLA
Ella is a 19 year-old sophomore in college, and attends Southern New Hampshire University as an English and Creative Writing major. She started writing poetry about a year ago. She has been struggling with PTSD, BPD, and MDD (Major Depressive Disorder), for most of her life, and from the age of seven until she was 15, she was in and out of mental hospitals, as well as residential behavioural facilities. Her grandparents took guardianship of Ella when she was seven, and stuck with her through it all, and continues to support her. She has just lost her uncle; it was her first bereavement and has hit her hard, but continues to write poetry.

Poetry by Chris Husband

HOW ARE YOU?

You ask me ....
"How are you?"
"Are you OK?"
Now what do I say?
I pause a beat ...

or two.
I don't think you can handle
the answer I want to give,
so, I give you the answer you expect.
"Fine thanks".

I'm currently questioning my sanity,
but my vanity won't disclose
the profanity in my head,
the inanity in my soul,
from the urbanity of my words.
Ask me again
and wait a beat ...

or two
and maybe you will get
an answer that is true

ABOUT THE POEM
"I wrote this poem as a response to the many times I have asked, and been asked 'How are you?' and just said or received the reply 'fine'. I realised that I very rarely give up anything about how I am really feeling, or expect anyone else to respond with more. I felt it belittled the meaning of the term and now try, wherever I can, to be more forthcoming. I feel that this situation is especially relevant to men when talking to each other and we have to learn to open up and be more available to each other."

ABOUT CHRIS
Chris is a poet and author from Lancashire, UK, who has written poetry on many different topics, from humorous, to serious and political, and a number touching on mental health issues that he has encountered himself and in his family. He has written two self-published poetry collections, and two children's picture books, and is

a keen open mic performer around Manchester, Liverpool and Lancashire.
W: www.chrishusband.com
FB: @chris.husband1
Twitter (X): @fgsgoose49
Instagram: @goosechris
Threads: @goosechris

My story (Anonymous)

I've struggled with my mental health in various ways throughout my life. I suffered with Selective Mutism from around age 3 to 7, which is an anxiety disorder, which means in circumstances of extreme anxiety I was physically unable to speak. I'm still unsure what the cause of it was, but it made my life very difficult as I could not communicate in school if I didn't understand something, or if I needed to use the toilet. My classmates did not understand my struggle as they were young and thought I didn't like them, and that I was choosing not to speak to them, when this was not the case.

I was referred to Speech and Language therapy after my diagnosis at around age six and began to use a voice recorder shared with my teacher. I don't personally recall this, but we had 'show and tell' during class, and I managed to pre-record a voice message saying "Happy Halloween" - or something of the equivalent, for the class. This exposure activity of letting the class hear my voice helped me overcome my Selective Mutism very quickly, and I was able to speak freely to whoever I wanted, but this isn't the case for everyone.

I progressed through primary school, and once I reached P7 (age 11-12), I started to struggle with my mental health again. We had to memorise Scottish poetry as a celebration leading up to Burns' Night, and my teacher was threatening to pick on someone if no one volunteered themselves. For some reason I volunteered myself - which was very out of character for me. As I stood in front of my awaiting classmates, I panicked. I knew what I wanted to say but I couldn't. My throat was excruciatingly sore and tight, and I couldn't get a single word out. I had not been told about my Selective Mutism, so I didn't know what was happening to me, and this really frightened me and I got really upset.

I have for the most part overcome my Selective Mutism, but this was a pivotal experience in my life, and to this day, I fear I may have another episode during presentations or high-pressure situations such as in emergencies.

P7 for me was the start of my poor mental health. I was struggling with friendships, and had extremely low self-esteem. I struggled in particular with my transition to secondary school, and had very high levels of anxiety. I recount many nights in my first year, crying as I didn't know what would happen, or what to expect of the next day. As a result, my parents decided to see if hypnotherapy would help me. At the time this was useful for me, but unfortunately after the sessions stopped, I continued my struggle with my mental health.

I really struggled with my school years and at around age 15 I sought external help from CAMHS mental health service. I was on their waiting list for over a year, and was then told I "did not meet the criteria". This was very disheartening – they hadn't even met me. This was arguably the start of my negative thoughts that I needed to get worse to be seen, heard, and be taken seriously.

Sometime after this my brother fell very ill and was hospitalised for three months with Guillain-Barré Syndrome. It was a very difficult time on all the family; my mum had to stay with him as he is autistic and mostly non-verbal (can't advocate for himself and didn't have much understanding of the situation). I was still having a rough time with my own mental health, and was even experiencing suicidal ideation, but I didn't want to burden my family as my brother - I felt at this time - was the priority. My mum in particular, at this time, was very distressed, and we would communicate to each other through cards we'd send. I'd go up and visit with my dad, but obviously we couldn't be there all the time.

Christmas day was the most difficult during this time. My dad and I stayed overnight in a visitor accommodation at the hospital. I didn't get much sleep. We tried our best, and so did the hospital, to have a normal day, but it just didn't feel the same. I struggled to eat in the hospital as it felt like a stressful environment, but I managed to eat microwaved spaghetti. I remember getting upset partially due to the situation, partly due to sleep deprivation. I then got very distressed as I was upset, and it was supposed to be a good day. I felt like I'd ruined Christmas. Luckily, the next month my brother was able to be discharged and he eventually - after lots of physiotherapy - learned to walk again after being paralysed from the waist down, and we could return to a sense of 'normality'.

Just a while after this time the pandemic started, and the country was in a state of lockdown. For many, the lockdowns were devastating, but for me they gave a sense of relief as school was not a safe place for me. For the first time I could finally ask questions through emails, and complete my work at my own pace, at whatever time I liked. My mental health started to improve and, as a result, so did my schoolwork.

There were parts of my life the pandemic negatively affected, such as my exams. Our exams were replaced with a closed book "assessment diet", which felt like a synonym for exams. We had very little notice, and I found out I had 21 assessments to complete within 4½ weeks. When I saw my assessment schedule (including eight assessments within a week) I just cried. We didn't have any study leave and still had to attend classes during this period, so I had to make time for myself to revise, which ate into my sleep. I would revise up until 4am.

After the assessments finished, I completely exhausted myself and became very ill. I lost my appetite completely, and the only thing that seemed slightly appealing was juice. I stayed in my bed and unintentionally ended up losing a lot of weight, though I didn't notice at the time. My parents were really concerned, and I remember feeling bad, but I couldn't help what I was going through. I revised so intensely that I ended up giving myself an eye condition. I ended up getting good results, however this was at the expense of my mental and physical health.

Once schools officially re-opened and things were "back to normal", I started to struggle again. I reached out to my school about needing extra support for my mental health, and I was told there's nothing more that could be done to help me, and there was a lot of invalidation and gaslighting surrounding experiences I brought to their attention. This was around the time I started to become truly impacted and traumatised by my ill-treatment from school.

This particular time is difficult for me to recall properly because of how much everything impacted me, but around this time I was having CBT privately. My therapist was very encouraging in terms of reaching out, but wasn't the best match as it didn't feel like she was acknowledging the weight of my experiences such as frightening intrusive thoughts and emotional dysregulation, which were both really overwhelming and unbearable for me. I would often sleep to escape my intense emotions as they were too much to handle.

My mental health was at its very worst. I was struggling with self-harm and suicidal ideation, along with many other things including dissociation and intense self-hatred. There was a point where I had around 40 intrusive thoughts within less than two weeks. I felt worthless and drained, and I was struggling with daily tasks such as brushing my teeth, wearing my glasses when I was supposed to, and preparing for the next day – laying out clothes and packing my bag. I had extremely strained relationships, which made me feel so alone. My teachers would yell at me for "not doing anything" when I was just trying to survive through the day. I often missed classes or taught myself because I just couldn't bare being at school being ostracised, excluded, and villainised for just existing.

One of my teachers said to me alone "I think you're ill and should go on medication". I had no idea how to react to that at 16 years old. I was shocked and kept this to myself for a day before telling my mum, who was rightly enraged, as she didn't know about this encounter at all. This was really damaging for me regardless of this teacher's intentions and from then on at school I was no longer myself. I was guarded, robotic, and didn't trust anyone. I wasn't myself anymore. I was like a ghost controlled by someone else to protect me. I started getting more dissociation episodes and flashbacks. I also had ongoing issues with skin picking which exacerbated due to my stress, leaving my fingers sore and raw.

There was one teacher, however, who I'm eternally grateful for. She was there for me at this time, even though she wasn't teaching me any classes. She listened to me, truly cared about me, and was always there for me. I would tell her about my day, what happened, how I was feeling, and she would help me through any emotional crisis' I was having. She also focused on solutions, which really helped me think about practicalities on how to deal with difficult experiences. She was there for me at my lowest points, but she also encouraged me and genuinely wanted the best for me, and would celebrate my wins, no matter how "small". The few things I left unsaid, I felt like she already knew, she felt like the first person that truly understood me, as much as another person could. She supported me through so much and I'm not sure I would be here today without her kindness and compassion.

In around October 2021, I had an extreme mental breakdown after a conflict. I felt so distressed and low, and I seriously wanted to end my life, on a much more intense level than ever before. I was hysterical and I had thoughts along the lines of "no one wants to see you live", "you're a burden, everyone would be so much happier", "it would be like an early Christmas present". My mum checked in on me when I was experiencing this extreme distress, and I told her the thoughts I was having. I can't recall her reaction, but I remember she asked if I thought I needed to be admitted and I responded, "I don't know". She then encouraged and helped me clean up my room a bit whilst listening to music.

There wasn't a lot that helped me during this time, but some things that eased the pain a little less were listening to music, therapy, and having someone to talk to that was empathetic and understanding.

In November 2021, when all of this was happening, I was diagnosed with social anxiety disorder. I thought this would help me be taken seriously at school, but unfortunately this wasn't the case. My mental health was so bad that I didn't think I would manage to do any exams, and I wasn't sure how far I'd make it when it was time for them anyway. I eventually did my prelims and got C's.

Something after that changed. I felt slightly better and was preparing for my exams, which took huge amounts of effort to catch up. I think this was around the time I applied for college and saw a way out. I applied for HND Social Sciences as I loved doing Higher Psychology. The requirements were 2 Highers, which seemed manageable.

My first true exams were my Highers because of the Covid

pandemic, which was extremely daunting as these were the ones that universities look at. I had accommodations in place for my social anxiety which helped (smaller room and extra time), however there were a few things that didn't go so well.

The exam schedule was very tight for individuals with extra time, so despite living in the same town as the school, I needed a taxi to get back in time for my second paper of a Biology exam. I was extremely distressed during an English exam, as there was a boy sat behind me who had consistently harassed me - and even sexually assaulted me throughout my time at this school. I became really upset and was hyperventilating in-between papers, and when I went to ask if I could change seats I was challenged and asked "why" despite being in a panicked, inconsolable state, and I was yelled at by the Deputy Head that said, "how old are you" and continued to yell other things I can no longer remember. Despite these setbacks, I got through my exams and left school with my Highers.

Once I left school, I felt like I finally had a life, I was no longer just surviving. Things started to look up and I finally realised that people don't just say "it gets better" to try and cheer people up, it can and does happen. I used to think I was the 'exception' to this saying as my life wasn't reflecting that at all, and I wasn't even sure if the saying was true. I realised I'm not the exception, but it takes time, and a huge amount of strength to wait and see it happen.

I'm currently in the process of seeking the appropriate help for my trauma, and trying to re-learn, and believe fully that there are good people out there as a part of my healing process. I received counselling, and I really struggled to come to terms with the fact that I have trauma from what I went through, as I still thought you had to experience something "truly" big like a car crash, when this isn't always the case, and I'm still working on validating myself and my experiences.

I started volunteering and, as a result, I've met some really kind and supportive people. I've also made good relationships with my lecturers and developed a firm level of trust in them. I've been doing well in my studies, and I now plan on going to university.

I still, at times, struggle with my mental health, but overall, I'm enjoying life surrounded by people who genuinely care about me, which makes the difficult times that little bit easier.

I hope my journey resonates with others and brings to light a glimpse of how mental health struggles vary in presentation and the impact they can have.

Poetry by Chris Langer

1—

late night
tossing and turning
the pill bottle

ABOUT THE POEM
*"This poem relates to both insomnia and depression. I often read and
re-read the pill bottles in an attempt to finally calm my mind for
rest."*

2—

therapy--
finding healing
in a strangers bed

ABOUT THE POEM
*"Trying to find respite from the past in a stranger's bed was my
method of healing, for better or worse, years ago."*

3—

in bed
too tired
to leave

ABOUT THE POEM
*"I believe many of us have felt the struggle of trying to leave bed on
particularly difficulty days."*

4—

television--
trying to escape
the news

ABOUT THE POEM
"The news can be so overwhelming with story after story of our

troubled world."

5—

side effects--
the cure
worse

ABOUT THE POEM
"Prescriptions to help with depression can intensify or exacerbate feelings. I wrote this haiku during a particularly difficult time after switching medications."

ABOUT CHRIS
Chris is a haiku poet currently residing in North Texas, USA. He is a survivor of depression of many years and owes his life to both his resolute friends and his cat, Cora. When not writing, he can be found reading a history book or exploring the outdoors.

Poetry by Alison Watson-Shields

WHAT DO YOU SEE?

What do you see, husband?
What do you see?
What do you think
When you're looking at me?

A fat, ugly woman
With greying hair and wrinkles
Skin sagging everywhere
Down pointing nipples

Thighs are like tree trunks
No gap to be seen
Big belly overhang
Where one piercings had been

Tired, dead eyes
That now see only pain
A downturned mouth
Will it ever smile again?

My brain is exhausted
From searching for clues
No positive thoughts
Just self mutilation and abuse

I cry in the mirror at these things that I see
A much larger shadow than the girl I used to be
No dregs of confidence, even with my degree
Is this what you see when you do look at me?

ABOUT THE POEM
"I am currently experiencing depression and anxiety, and this poem is about my own insecurities, and struggles with how I see myself."

STILL ME

I am the same person, only different
I wonder where all of this came from
I hear things but I don't understand

I see what is directly in front without depth
I want to be heard and understood

I am the same person, only different
I pretend to do what I once could but I can't
I feel curios but need you to keep me safe
I touch, reach out but I cannot judge depth
I worry that you think I am crazy, a burden
I cry because I am angry, frustrated and anxious

I am the same person, only different
I say things with mime and gesture, please listen to me
I dream and get stuck in episodes from my life
I try to control my life but have become over-reliant
I hope you understand I am having a hard time.

I am the same person, only different
I like music, rhythm, clapping and swearing
I believe in my own reality
I realise it may differ from yours
I live in the past, in my memories
I can still do many things, just not like I used to

I am the same person, only different.
I understand that there is more to me than this disease but do you?

ABOUT THE POEM
"This poem is written from the perspective of a person living with dementia, inspired by my role in caring for my grandmother who was diagnosed with Dementia with Lewy bodies in 2015, and how she changed as the disease progressed."

Poetry by Nadia Martelli

SPLIT

Have you ever heard the one
About the girl who learned a song
About a severance, bond undone?
No doubt she burned and yearned too long,
To answer questions, to understand
The fancy lessons, the second hand
Been dealt to others, not as planned;
But she discovered forgotten lands,
Where she was light, where she ran free
In pure delight, where none could see
Her plea, her plight, who she could be -
Her core not fighting, now She is We,
For I am Her, that little girl
So lost and scared, head in a whirl;
Did no-one care that She'd been hurled
From Innocence to a shattered world,
Where She was forced to look away,
Had to pretend She liked to play
His game of Kiss, Don't Tell, Don't Say -
She had to split that part away...

KEEP THEM

I'd like to introduce you to the Ones that live Inside,
My split personalities who no longer wish to hide,
There is Me, plus twelve of Them, each One is unique;
So, let's see which of Them will emerge, and dare to speak:

Hi, my name is BLUE, and I'm the One that's always there,
Making sure we function, in a way that's real, and fair,
Helping with the daily chores, the challenges at hand,
Dealing with Officialdom We don't all understand.

Hi, SINEAD, aged 22, the damaged, grown-up girl,
Who's learned some way to make it through, in this duplicitous world,
I may not be the healthiest, the best at keeping safe,
But I front for Us most of the time, only resting in Our Faith.

Hi, I'm CHARLIE, (Charlotte), and I absorbed the pain

And trauma She was living through, driving Her insane,
Though I'm just 11, I am wise beyond my years,
I come out if She needs Me to split-off from present fears.

My name is CHRISTOPHER, bearer of the shield
And sword used to protect Us, I'm the fighter in the field,
No-one passes In or Out without coming to me,
And I decide optimum ways to let Them feel They're free.

We are JADE & TONI, twins, never apart,
We're the balance in the Chaos, protecting Her heart
From breaking even further, so We act out, misbehave,
But all with good intentions as, Our Truth, We try to save.

There are no more Others who can share yet, find a voice,
With many secrets to uncover, They're still trying to make a choice,
To speak their Sin, their stories of the treasures they have lost,
So bleak within Their world, They're still reeling from the cost.

I hope you know Us better, that you see all we have known,
And that you will endeavour to acknowledge all We've shown;
I'm glad Some spoke out loud enough for somebody to hear,
And learn some of the reasons why I must keep Them so near.

ABOUT THE POMS
"I wrote these poems about my Dissociative Identity Disorder in order to raise awareness of the illness and it's symptoms."

ABOUT NADIA
Nadia is a 50-something poet, musician and artist. Born and raised in Liverpool, they relocated to the East Midlands, aged 18, to attend University. There, they gained a degree in Combined Arts, staying in the area after joining a local band as drummer, backing vocalist and songwriter, and still lives there today. They began writing person-centred poetry from an early age, and has been honing their unique style ever since. Nadia's dream is to publish a collection of their own poetry, and this is a step towards that calling.

Poetry & Prose by Danelle Cheney

SUNFLOWER

The hazy, late-day sun, wild and high,
Creates a lofty, other-world sunflower
That walks and won't say goodbye.
Repelled, I crouch, crawl and cower.

I try to shoot an arrow,
Mangle the overwhelming cheer;
I dwell in the dark and narrow,
A spiked wheel, parked in fear.

Leafy green feet, sunglasses tilted,
the cheerful sunflower sings my name,
And I feel stagnated, stilted,
Wadded up like a ball of shame.

Away, I cry, depart, and disappear!
The sunflower pauses, plucks off a leaf,
Gives it to me and shimmers with tears.
I drop the leaf, and cry with disbelief:

I can't cheer up, just leave me alone!
The sunflower's tears fall on my feet,
They glisten as I blink and groan,
And walk along the dusty street.

As I walk, the street floods with tears,
I hear laughter, singing, and joyful noise
And soon the water comes up to my ears.
I rise, wet and stunned, among convoys.

I'm on a ship surrounded by other ships;
I see armed defense at every corner,
Support and refuge tingle in my fingertips,
Strength trickles into my eroded armor.

Soon the sunflower's enormous face
Leans its posh stem over the ship's bow
The remnants from the tears' trace
Form pearly lines on white petals somehow.

The sunflower disappears, Poof! It leaves
pearly lines, traces of yesterday,
An amazing love that I receive,
A salve of grace on my hands that I raise.

SIREN

The encouragement of a spring snowstorm bends the pine branches
and almost breaks the limbs. I shiver even as the rays of sun thaw
the drifts, as the wind's hand

takes snow off the pine trees, throws it into the air, and scatters puffs
as if from a white dandelion. I watch it and wish for lucidity, for the
wind's hand to blow the misery away.

If madness has another name, it might be a siren, one that alerts
everyone that it clutches victims with a desperate fist. It alerts
everyone but me, the madwoman who does not know she's mad.
Until it's too late. I throw snowballs at myself, some of them rock
hard because I hate this madness, this epiphany that echoes in the
night and tells

me what it is. The hardship holds me in handcuffs. The rocking chair
beckons to me with the fuzzy gray blanket and I rock with my
handcuffed hands. I watch through the window at a woman with
white hair who walks down the street in the cold with a red plaid wool
shawl, heavy, that falls to her knees. She pushes a stroller with little
feet that kick up and down.

Every day, morning and before dusk, the same woman walks by. The
child's feet grow bigger and soon a bigger stroller is required and the
woman now wears a light blue jacket. Back and forth, back and forth,
until the sun rises earlier and sets later, and the marigolds and
bluebells bloom. Now that it's summer, the heat rises from the wet

asphalt after the rain stops. Then the sprinkler from the sky turns off,
and is silent, a dry sponge. The forest fires rage in different areas of
Colorado. The alarm of the fire news startles me out of the rocking
chair to outside. I walk beside different lots where the wind blows
through crested wheatgrass, Canadian thistle, and fescue grass and
the sun

beams through Douglas firs. I follow the woman with the stroller back
and forth, back and forth, from sunrises to sunsets, until the child

grows into a young man with dark red hair who can reach up and touch tree branches high into the air until he drives off into the shaded highways to grow into his own life.

I become the woman who I follow with leaves in my white hair, who takes medicine made out of tarragon, drinks lemon balm tea, notices the details of the rocks on the ground, and studies the shoes on my feet, worn and battered, that once staggered, but now can travel without fear.

ABOUT THE PIECE
"The 'I' is me."

I WANT TO BE YOUR RIVER

The road through the forest is a river, a blue sprawling jewel in the sun. They follow it, gaze into it as it splashes through the trees. They ask the river "Am I a man or woman?" and kneel beside its coldness. The answer rises in wind chime language harmonized with the river's gurgle. They listen to the refrain and ask, "What does it mean?" And find that neither man nor woman fits how they feel. They ask the river, "Do I have to be either one?" They grasp for freedom to be neither, a kind of pendulum that swings back and forth but stops at infinite points in between. As their mother, I hold the pendulum, follow its movements, and ask "Why?" Silence, broken words, and an unknown cause strangle the answer. Still, I point to what I think it is and stand with the rest of the family on unstable ground. The wobbly, wooden planks of undiagnosed manic depression and a marriage that does not know how to keep a steady rhythm is an alien who shoots black arrows. We attempt to dodge the arrows but slip into deep mud along the way. At first, we can't see our reflection in the mud but gradually begin to create tunnels that lead to our hearts. We may eventually use our hands to form objects of renewal in the mud: vases that hold life-changing water, book covers with "miracles" embossed that contain stories of transformation. Perhaps my child lives in part as an answer to pain like many do. They stay in a comfortable place that doesn't make them dig tunnels to their heart. Maybe someday they'll be able to answer the door when pain knocks, cover pain with a soft knitted blanket, unravel it and let it fall to the floor, and finally step on it with their whole weight. Their defined identity may change or may continue. It is most important for them to hold a mirror, tell the truth, accept what has led to this identity, and see threads of joy weave through their body as recognition, open arms, and self-love alleviate the pain buried within. The rush of the river is their growth. My hand holds theirs tighter, but they break free as expected. In the river, rocks form a path, a crazy jointed rope, which spells their name. I want to be a river so that I can support the rapids that help their sorrows drift away, and bear the ebullient waters that hold their dreams.

ABOUT THE PIECE
"This piece is about me as a mother"

ABOUT DANELLE
Danelle writes from Colorado, USA, and is a poet, artist, and podcaster who seeks to inspire resilience for those with troubled minds like bipolar. As a Bipolar I Disorder sufferer, she has an empathy and awareness of how mental illness can take a toll. With an undergraduate degree in Creative Writing, and advanced degrees in Journalism and Human Communication Studies, she brings a story-like quality to her poetry, with elements of magic realism and fantasy, while at the same time, addressing the authentic pain and joy and sorrow - the vast array of emotions - that we all experience. Before marriage and children, she taught in colleges as a communications and writing instructor in a variety of subjects within the field which include conflict and communication, public speaking, interpersonal communication, and business writing. Her most notable professorship was at a local, esteemed engineering college where she won grants to support social science research on gender influence in teams.
Instagram: @danelacates

Sarada Gray's story

Communing with Cohen: a Memoir of Forgetting on my experience of going through the menopause

I'd walked to the Infirmary a thousand times. Having lived in this city for thirty years I knew every street and back-alley, every corner shop and sweet centre, every furniture emporium and graffitied underpass. Like a London cabbie I could have taken you anywhere in the city if required, and had the whole of Leicester been flattened I could have rebuilt it stone by stone. How could I ever lose my way?

As I set off for the hospital I inserted my earphones and selected *Songs of Leonard Cohen*. Cohen first came into my life when I was fourteen, when a student teacher put on a scratchy record and Suzanne filled the room. I was hooked: I got the album, I went to the concert; I learned to strum the songs. The man has been a weird sort of guru to me ever since those days – I just never anticipated how that might play out.

It should have been a twenty-minute stroll, once you factor in the inevitable miles of corridor inside the hospital. Even so I felt privileged to live within walking distance when so many people had to travel right across the county and sit in a queue of cars sniffing each others tails and waiting for admittance to the car park. To be anxious about an operation would add insult to this injury, but for me this was a routine appointment, a routine journey. As I started off confidently down the street Suzanne strummed quietly, the man's gravelly voice working its magic and helping me forget the traffic. I pressed the button at the crossing and as I waited for the green man without any warning my mind stalled. I looked up the road; I looked to left and right. Which way was it? How could I not remember? The lights changed and I stood immobile as the cars flew by and walkers pushed irritably past. What was happening? Suddenly the streets were foreign to me, as if I'd been lifted up and plonked down in a strange city. Aptly enough, Cohen's *Stranger Song* twanged in my ears, singing of a forty-year-old loneliness. A smartphone would have helped but they had yet to become affordable; in the end I got out my ancient Nokia and rang my husband. I was in tears: what on earth should I tell him? I felt utterly stupid and I couldn't explain what was happening.

If I had chosen a life partner with just this situation in mind I could not have done better. He gently talked me through the route and I wrote it all down. Following his directions like a tourist, I got to the hospital and even managed to find the right room for my appointment, which went without a hitch. I made it home again without too much trouble and by the evening I was beginning to shrug the whole thing off. It was just a blip, that's all. A momentary lapse. Low blood sugar? Maybe. A good dinner, a sound sleep and the whole thing would be forgotten.

But the next day it happened again. And again. Every time I walked out of the door it was the same; my memory would light the way for a few minutes and then descend into fog. I took to bringing a street map with me and hoping desperately that no-one I knew would spot me looking at it. What on earth would I tell them? How could I explain that all the geography in my head had been erased and that where my mental maps should be there was simply a thick fog?

All this was bad enough but worse was to come. Soon I started forgetting people. I'd recognise a face but not give it a name – or put the wrong name to a face. I'd forget everything I knew about them. Where did we meet? How did I know them? How *well* did I know them – were we friends or mere acquaintances? *Did* I know them, or was I saying hello to complete strangers? And what if they stopped to chat? What if I said, *how's your husband?* only to be told that I went to his funeral last month? What if I blurted out "I don't know when I last saw Richard!" only to be told that I'd seen him last Christmas? I resorted to smiling and making bland conversation, hoping desperately that nothing awkward would come up.

But this was not all. Soon I lost my sense of smell; where scents should be there was a blank like the fog in my head. I tried kick-starting it with essential oils but to no avail: a gas leak and a bunch of lavender would leave me equally unmoved.

I lost swathes of my own life too: holidays with the children, films with my husband, anniversary meals, concerts – they all went. It got so that I couldn't trust my own mind any more and this led to terrible chasms of self-doubt – if you can't trust your own mind what can you trust? It was like living with dementia: every day brought more loss.

Then the Episodes began.

Though I've never been a brilliant sleeper I normally stay in bed at least until seven – but now I'd be wide awake at three, a full-blown, adrenaline-fuelled daytime consciousness which propelled me out of bed. Once up, I started feeling an irresistible urge to meditate.

I'd practised meditation for twenty years but in moderation: ten minutes morning and night, if at all. But now I sat down and meditated for hours, right till the sun rose – and these meditations were the most vivid I've ever experienced.

I can call all this it by its name now; I can own it, but at the time I had no idea what was happening. All I knew was that in this state of deep meditation I believed I was communing with Leonard

Cohen – and as the days went by and the meditation grew deeper I became convinced that he was going to enter my life and transform it. As my fifty-second year passed I waited for something to happen – but nothing did.

The weeks went on, every day the same. No-one said the word psychosis.

For every up there is a down. Every swing comes back to earth; every see has a saw – and after a while fatigue began to hit me mid-afternoon, after which I'd be plunged into a deep depression. Like Cohen in his worst moods I tasted utter desolation. I felt I had nowhere to turn, that my life was worthless and pointless. This went on for a few hours; then in the evening I would gradually come to myself. After that I'd go to bed and the whole cycle would start again. No-one said the word *bipolar*. And then it occurred to me: in the last three months I had not had a single period.

All I'd ever heard about the menopause was the stereotypical hot flush. Strip off the bedclothes, open the windows and try not to feel self-conscious about resembling a slow-motion belisha beacon. It never occurred to me that the menopause could trigger memory loss, let alone psychosis. But now I was onto something. I began to do some research: I found that I was not alone, that thousands, maybe millions of women experience memory loss in menopause. It's very common to experience mental health problems too – if only I'd known!

In time the episodes passed and with them the depression. Perhaps I should have gone to the doctor, but I didn't – rightly or wrongly I've always been reluctant to medicalise my mental health problems, believing that they have something to teach me. This proved to be a period of transition, not only from middle-age to getting older but from one career to another. I decided that now was the time to devote my whole life to something I'd wanted to do since I was eight: I retired from teaching and I began to write full-time. This I have never regretted.

Fifteen years on, the picture is patchy. I still have no sense of smell, and though it's improved the memory fog persists. I rely on smartphones and satnav to get around and my husband is my own personal historian. I have diaries I can consult, and a blog where I can check what I've been up to. I don't commune with Leonard Cohen any more (especially since he's dead) but sometimes psychosis will sweep over me like a dissolve in a film so that I feel I'm losing my hold on reality. I've learned some techniques now to deal with it and by and large it passes: I just have to stop what I'm doing, let the world pass me by and count everything I can see and hear. With all these things at my disposal I get by; sometimes I even do more than get by. Sometimes I pass for normal.

I hate misery memoirs, which is why this isn't one. Menopause is part of the cycle of life; I'm glad I was able to have children and I'm glad I don't have periods any more, but so much of my suffering could have been saved if I'd had more information about the process. If I'd known that memory loss and mental health problems and even psychosis were common experiences it would have saved so much of the pain, confusion and sheer terror of not knowing what was happening. In that spirit I offer this memoir, in the hope that it may save others too.

ABOUT SARANDA

Sarada started writing stories and poems at the age of eight and has been published in magazines such as *Mslexia, Everyday Fiction* and *What the Dickens*. She was poet in residence at Sound Cafe - a homeless project in Leicester, and has performed in such diverse places as Leicester Cathedral and The Fourth Plinth in Trafalgar Square. She also write radio plays.

Blog: https://lizardyoga.wordpress.com

Poetry by Karla Linn Merrifield

INDEPENDENCE MOMENT

Pack it away
in Styrofoam curls,
bubble-wrap, yesterday's
newspapers. Pack it away
in boxes, better yet, pages
of journals on shelves twenty,
thirty volumes wide. Pack it
away in dusty photo albums,
in sleeves of prints never even
sorted or labeled with dates. Pack
past lives, past wives & husbands,
away in nerve cells at the back
of the brain locked in unconsciousness.
Pack the past away for another day
of loneliness, discovery, & lovely uncovery;
for other nights of timelessness alone
just on the edge of sightless nights
& memory about to fade to death.

I'm still barefoot, braless, brave
enough to take more pictures,
write thousands of lines, maybe millions
word by word, minute by minute: Now.

SCATTERED

Bones of my left hand rattle
in the cup of a sideshow soothsayer.

Marrow of thigh bones – sturdy femurs they were –
is rich picking for western ravens.

A shaman (I can't see his face) beats
a deerskin drum with my tibias and fibias.

My skull, its twin sockets, emits
candlelight for a poet to write by.

Ribs shape a lucky friend's new creel holding

a dozen rainbow trout for dinner.

And the man who was once my beloved
kisses my sternum yet, remembering my breasts.

But the rest of my remains are dust blown
on the trade winds: waiting for you to inhale.

THE PLACE OF PURPOSE

A day at my disposal I spend
to remember again this is for keeps;
you are married to a mystery.

I am fully employed as hard laborer
as in cane fields, earning my payload
of words penetrating boredom's burden.

Even when frozen fingers must thaw
the disappearing ink, even when sun-scabbed hands
must salvage the page of ephemerality,

I show up. I show up on Time,
knotted nylon socks as a headband against
salt of perspiration, of tears in my eyes.

On ice, in fire, muscular lines stir cauldrons
of fuel and syrup to illuminate sweetened dreams

ABOUT KARLA
Karla has had 1000+ poems appear in dozens of journals and
anthologies. She also has 16 books to her credit. Following her 2018
Psyche's Scroll (Poetry Box Select) is the full-length book *Athabaskan
Fractal: Poems of the Far North from Cirque Press.* Her newest poetry
collection, *My Body the Guitar,* nominated for the 2022 National Book
Award, was inspired by famous guitarists and their guitars. She is
also a frequent contributor to *The Songs of Eretz Poetry Review.*
W: www.karlalinnmerrifield.org
FB: @karlalinn.merrifield
Blog: karlalinnmerrifield.wordpress.com
X: @LinnMerrifiel

Poetry by Pam Ski

MY BROTHER PETE

Such a good-looking bloke,
But his life was traumatic,
Bipolar ... it's no flipping joke.

University didn't go well,
Crashed 'n' burned twice,
Poor old mum ... it was hell.

Then ... sort of all right ... for a bit,
Qualified as an accountant
Before ... his career hit the skids.

Back then, the law gave no protection ...
And companies get nervous when
You keep on being sectioned.

Life was tough on his own,
Too difficult to live with ...
But ... at least he had a home.

He used his brains 'n' creativity
To save the local rugby club ...
A focus for his abilities.

He developed diabetes,
Couldn't quit the cigs or booze
Succumbed to heart disease.

Such a good-looking bloke,
But his life was traumatic,
Bipolar ... it's no flipping joke.

ABOUT THE POEM
"A couple of days ago, I came across a photo of my brother, Pete (taken in his mid 50s) and felt that I wanted to write about his struggle with bipolar.In 1967 he suffered a psychotic episode and was diagnosed with manic depression - the old term for bipolar. He was a young man of 21, studying for a degree in economics at Keele

University. The first episode was dramatic, and he was hospitalised for a long time. I was seven years old when it happened. After he recovered, he worked at Midland Bank for a few years, but against my parents wishes, he went back to Keele for another try. The party lifestyle didn't do him any favours, and he had another breakdown. Not only was Pete in and out of psychiatric units over his lifetime, but the stress triggered my mum - who had a milder form of bipolar - to have psychotic episodes as well. They were both lovely people and they went through hell. Pete died in 2004 aged 59 from a major heart attack."

Poetry by Becky Topham

YOUR GIFT
(For Alfie, my son)

When I saw your smile today
I forgot that my mind is broken
I forgot the black of blackness
And all the painful words spoken

When I saw your smile today
My spirit lifted high
Up past the storm clouds
I saw such life in your eye

When I saw your smile today
I made a promise to myself
You are not here to heal me
I must do that all by myself

Your smile is such a balm
Your giggle like a thousand bubbles
And when I hear it echoing
I am devoid of all my troubles

MOTHER
(For Alfie)

I don't feel that I deserve you
Little man in blue

What is mother? Who is she?...
She is the person I am desperate to be

Do I bring you love, routine and joy?
My beautiful, precocious little boy

Am I mother? Am I enough?
Bipolar and motherhood can be tough

Yet, despite all the days ofI doubt
At least I may say aloud

I am mother ... I am mother
And I wish to be no other.

FIGHT

On the darkest day of my life
When I was saturated with fear
I found something grand inside of me
Missing for many years

This illness has left me bereft
And without a coat of armour
Yet, suddenly I realised
I was about to reach the harbour

For all the waves and salt wind
For all the ardent clinging on
I realised my own pure strength-
It had been there all along

Amidst those screaming storm clouds
I recognised my fight
It was there within my reach
Where day meets the blackest night

And so, I learnt to conquer
To stand tall and upright
I will no longer fear tomorrow
Or the dawning of its light

THE MADNESS

This flamboyant soul
Is often intertwined
With euphoric excess
And crisp white wine

It loves a party
It loves to chatter
The subject negligible
It doesn't matter

Mania is fun

The world exciting and unknown,
The sad thing is..
I experience it all alone

And it drives away
Those I adore
Whispers and reprimands
The slam of a door

Depression my nemesis
Is an unrelenting square
Of blackest black
A self constructed lair

It staggers beside me
A beggar of sorts
Extracting from me
All positive thoughts

Yet, I am so much more
Than bipolar disorder
Try to see me first
In this very order:

I am a mum
A wife and nurse
Loyal friend and colleague
These blessings come first

THE HORROR MOVIE
(Bipolar)

Like watching a horror movie
Inside my own chest,
My heart the spectator
And its beat has no rest

Constant self hatred
And impending doom
And then,suddenly- sunshine
It arrives with a boom

And my voice, I hear it,
Chattering away

I can't get a word in
It demands its say

Everything sparkling
And oh the laughter!
And we shall all live
Happily ever after!

Two extremes
Sometimes two for one!
Mania I miss you
When you are gone

But depression, I hate you
You smother this soul
Yet,two halves of this illness
Make one unique whole

ABOUT THE POEMS
"I have bipolar affective disorder. I have struggled in many ways with my diagnosis, but have found some empowerment in writing. My poetry is a journal of sorts. It enables me to pull myself out of the most difficult of times. However, it is important to note that writing alone is not enough to control this disorder and I am finally medicated therapeutically. I know, from absolute raw experience, that words heal. And I wish all sufferers of mental health disorders the strength to fight"

ABOUT REBECCA
Rebecca is a 43 year-old staff nurse from Yorkshire. She is the author of *My Mask*.

Poetry by Lucy Simms

UNFATHOMABLE DEPTHS

I watch helplessly from the window,
As the chopper, with mournful drone, hovers overhead.
The waiting is interminable;
Unbearable.
The liaison officer
Ensures I remain, not flee to find you.

The table, with your abandoned keys is evidence
You do not intend to return.
A grim reality, that happens to others.

The search shifted out to sea:
That magnet to the distressed
Frantic radio communication
Said you had been found.

Plucked from the devouring sea,
Wading towards a horizon you would never reach.
Helpless against the powerful churnings of your mind;
That darkest abyss, with its demons of despair,
Making death seductive.

Did you resent being saved?
Was I selfish burdening you with living?
It is hard not to pick at the scars
Seared into our souls.

Perhaps we could head
Towards a brighter horizon,
Negotiating the storms together?

I want you here,
But it has to be what you want too.

ABOUT THE POEM
*"This poem describes the time after the attempted suicide of a bipolar
friend, and how I became the carer and gave up work to be on
suicide watch; together with the invaluable help of the mental health
team. I felt totally unprepared, but did my best to cope as it was
definitely not about me. The fear of it happening again has never left*

me however, and I wonder if it ever will. It is a burden so many of us must carry. I am happy to say my friend has made good progress; but like anyone - has good and bad days. I have learnt so much and am just so grateful I was able to help, and that the police listened; taking my fears seriously."

ABOUT LUCY
A few years ago, Lucy moved from the north to the south coast of the UK to fulfil her dream of living near the sea. It was a huge gamble, as she knew nobody. But from volunteering, and her self-employment as a tutor, she quickly settled and made new friends. After researching her ancestors and finding they also lived here centuries ago, it was definitely one of her better decisions and, as an adopted person, this meant so much and really felt like coming home.

Poetry by Boakesey

FOOLING EVERYONE

We first met him the Sunday after we'd moved house
Our old church too far away
We opted for the nearest
and there he was, to greet us
Not the Vicar, or the Curate
But as this was a daughter church
in a small rural village
this was *his* domain.
Not even God's

Organist, churchwarden, choir-
master and Sunday School leader
He *was* the church.
Before long, my Gran was singing his praises
She could write a hymnal
Jam-packed with all the wonderful
deeds and kindnesses he'd done,
Welcoming us to the community.

My mother was less impressed.
I think.
But then, she was busy battling her Demons
Bipolar and alcoholic
Her daily fight was fooling folk
that she was well enough to teach.
Until the day she fell apart
Had to go 'away'.

Our Saviour stepped up to the mark
Lifts to hospital, shopping runs
Daily visits to our home
And when the Xmas Concert neared
a soloist was selected.
Yours truly.
Away in a Manger
Chosen for a duet too – with The Man Himself
Good King Wenceslas. I was the Page.
Lots of rehearsing required, of course.
I've hated Xmas ever since
Away in the Danger

It's the time I learned to fool the World
Just as he'd fooled us and everyone else.
I dared not tell a single soul
Not even the God
I no longer believed in
Five years it lasted. Every time
I tried to stop it, he'd remind me
of my Gran's weak heart
She'd never cope with the shock
I'd be responsible for her death
Fool that I was.
I fell for his lies
But then, I was only twelve.

ABOUT THE POEM
*"I've tried not to be too specific in this poem, but yes, I am a survivor
of child abuse. My abuser died before it could get to court so I'll
never get Justice, but writing this piece and Writing for Well-Being in
general has been the key to my being able to process the traumas of
my younger years."*

PAVING STONES

Paving stones
Cracks between them.

Heavy with my cares upon my shoulders
Each step I take
Another shattered stone
More & more gaps
Between damaged shards
For me to slip
And fall
And fall
And fall...

Maybe this writing practice
Will be my mortar
Gluing back together
The fragments of my self
Like crazy-paving slabs
A broken being
Trying to keep myself
Together

Together
Together...

ABOUT THE POEM
"This was one of the earliest poems I wrote as I started my Writing for Well-Being journey and discovered the sheer power of words to heal and build resilience, when used by a trained facilitator."

STICKS AND STONES

"Sticks and stones may break my bones
But words can never hurt me"
What genius came up with that?
The world's worst advice ever.
When the bullies came for me,
The bruises all healed rapidly
And, since the teachers never saw
A single thing, to prove my truth
Powerless to help, or just unwilling.
Being left out hurt – a lot
But nothing like the hateful names:
"Stinky", "fatty", I'd ignore
The worst came when I reached my home
A sanctuary? Don't make me laugh!
Those labels festered all my life:
"Fatherless b@st@rd", "Devil spawn"
From the Gran that I should love.
The words cut deep, controlling me.
But the ultimate, cruellest, was my mum
Explaining how, when I was born
My twin did not survive at all.
My cord was wrapped around his neck
No good would EVER come of me
For killing my brother with my first breath

ABOUT THE POEM
"Family members can be really cruel to each other, sometimes accidentally, often intentionally. My grandmother bullied and berated my mother every day of her life for having a child out of wedlock, not realising (I hope) that I could hear every word of her bigoted rants. When my mother was unwell, she took it out on me. Is it any wonder that I had zero self-esteem for years and was easy prey for a predatory paedophile? Writing pieces like this are cathartic and empowering. It can be challenging at the time of writing, so choosing

what to write about and when is vitally important."

ABOUT BOAKESEY
Recently inaugurated as the ninth official Manx Bard, Boakesey was born illegitimate. Her family has a history of mental health issues: her father had episodes of depression; her mother was bipolar and an alcoholic, and died of an overdose when she was fifteen. Boakesey became the target of a paedophile which resulted in her PTSD and several episodes of depression, including quite a few genuine suicide attempts. Thankfully, CBT and *Writing for Well-Being* saved her. She had to give up work in 2018 due to a series of strokes, which left her mobility impaired. However, she is not ready to retire, so has enrolled on a Creative Writing and Therapy MA, so she can use the power of words to help others on their healing journey.

Poetry by Daniel William Zampino

A DREAM SO VIVID

Sometimes a dream is so vivid it seems inescapable.
With the gentle apprehension
of morning, I'm reminded of the saying
of an anonymous rabbi, thousands of years ago,
foretelling that
all life is unfathomable.
A woman, a girl I hadn't thought of for forty years,
stalks my dreams and now my daylight. Haunting in her friendly
stare.
In the dream I shield her from harm, listen to whatever she is saying.
Flashing her blue eyes, buried under thick framed glasses,
She's the most intelligent girl in the class.
Endearing with a gentle smile.
But who is she?
All life is unfathomable.
Barely knew her when I did, fragile presence she bears,
and I'm protective, the wordlessness ensconced in her
plain prettiness that leaves me unprepared for the invasive thought.
She had killed herself.
Forty years ago.

Stalking my wakefulness with her genial glare.
Unforgivable.
She truly hated herself.

Why this nighttime visit?
A sacrilege?
Do I control who enters my dreams?
All life is unfathomable.
I barely knew her.
But where was I when she lay dying? – demanding of me my solace?
        Or was her showing up in my dream purely happenstance?

I hadn't thought of her for forty years.
Her father proclaimed someday she'd be president, or a great concert
pianist.
But didn't he assault her elder sister (physically) in her presence? –
        She hated her father for the way she was praised.
Her survival was her stain.
Still the piano keys purred when she played.

But she never made it to the Boston Symphony, did she?

She lived in her homely gait until the day she spruced up,
when she mushroomed into a spring flower miming a debutant.
She was a caterpillar sprouting butterflying wings.
Her suitor, tall and handsome, suit, tie, and overcoat,
endowed her with romanticism. She never looked so alive.
But isn't this what dreams are made of? –

Desperate in her belief that life was wonderful,
Yet when the garment of love was removed,
        her gallant lover had to face
        the cauldron of her ire.
A maimed butterfly, she hated her father, and his great expectations.
She hated herself for hating her father.
Fate, that unpalatable goddess,
        foretold
        her life would end badly.

The stinging verse of her ire,
seized from her father's violence,
made her unbearable.
Her lover's kindness, rewarded with fury,
destined his removal.
The terror of her aloneness had turned bottomless.

Uncanny that she would seep,
like floating driftwood,
into my night –
as I was forced to ask
who was she?
        A madame president?
        A concert pianist?
        A jilted lover?
Life is unfathomable.

Was it the gentleness of her smile that seduced me,
or the scream of her suicide?

ABOUT THE POEM
"For seven years I worked at McLean Hospital, Belmont, USA, during
the late 1970s and early 1980s, spending three and a half years on a
unit for long-term care. Such units, seen today as outmoded, or
rather too expensive, brought in a 'milieu' setting patients and staff
as a kind of 'family' - but there was a lot of hidden tragedy which we

(as staff) came in contact with. This poem reflects a dream I had of one of the patients I worked with, and how her memory (specifically the memory of her suicide) emerged in my dream-unconscious. The poem is a simple recap of what I dreamed, and its aftermath."

Poetry by Eleanor Laurel

INTRO TO MY JOURNEY

Tears from the sky kiss the earth.
Raindrops pouring,
Wind roaring.
Every moment in this storm is worth
Seeing the morning tomorrow.
The flowers of summer
Are paid for with spring bummers.
Joy must borrow from sorrow.
Like the sky, my soul is full of clouds.
An impenetrable darkness that won't go
And only occasionally allows light to show.
But most often, my heart they enshroud.
I can't shake this loneliness.
It is so deep, so wide
I know not where to hide,
Which causes me vast distress.
Don't take me wrong,
I know I'm cared for and loved.
But from love, I feel so intensely unplugged.
There is nowhere I really belong.
On this great journey of life,
I feel like there's someone missing.
Something gone that keeps me wishing
For hope, freedom, death or knife.
Anything to keep me from feeling
Like I do right now.
Somehow,
I have to find healing.
My heart grieves for a lost loved one
Who is forever gone.
But now truths rise with the dawn.
That story never was, so it's not done.
I grieve a person I never met.
Someone I could never love or hate.
Though they never existed, these feelings still don't abate.
I wonder if they're forever set.
Will I always miss a loved one who's never been there
To care?
Do I want someone fair
To hear my story, with all my experiences to share?

I am deeply wounded by this situation
For it cannot be fixed.
My life seems nixed.
I always fall for evil's insinuation.
Although I am a certain mess,
I do want hope.
I want a good life-scope.
There is something left fighting in me, I will confess.
So, come join me on my journey.
It will be interesting and lovely,
And sometimes sad and ugly.
But I will win the tourney.

***

ABOUT THE POEM
"Occasionally I try to describe
My journey and the way I fight.
Because putting my darkness in the light
Has the power to silence my mind's cruel gibe"

TWOFOLD

The years I don't count
Are the years I spent drowning.
Each day a decade,
And every moment a million hours.
Until, with my last strength,
My cries finally found audience
And that fateful hand with luster glorious
Sought to pull me from the deep.
If only I had known the burn of the icy air.
And the agony of lungs previously deprived
Being swallowed in the sharp vastness
Of the atmosphere.
How could I know, that the hands which reached into my prison
to set me free
Waited to whisk the breath from my frozen lips?
I grasped that last hope
Because I thought the pain could end.
But this hurts too,
In a different way.
Maybe worse.
How do you compare smothering

To an agony of burning?
I sit here under the bright sky
Looking at those deceptively sparkling waters
Knowing many drown there.
Knowing I too should have been deprived of air.
It stabs my heart to know I was spared
When others drowned by breathing impaired.

***

ABOUT THE POEM
"Though I escaped the tragedy of suicide
With the help of intervention,
I know I should have perished
And I feel guilt for those who do,
Because I got the help they didn't."

APOLOGY TO MYSELF

If one were to pry the depths of my mind
I'm certain they would find
Darkness and evils of all kinds.
The depth of my own brokenness even I do not know.
For I refuse the mirror
In fear that my true colors will show.
How is it that death is so attractive
when it is contrary to life,
For which we were made?
If pleasure is sought,
And pain is fought,
Why do knives and blades call my name?
It must be, that deep in my soul,
There are cavities, crevices, wounds and holes.
They long for the surface.
To the skin they must rise,
Else I have no healing purpose,
And only more sorrow can I devise.
Jess, I'm so sorry you got stuck with this darkness.
You are so beautiful.
You are strong, you are loving.
You are free.
But because you are part of me
These parts of you, I'll never see.
I loathe these injuries; the blackness I hold.

But it calls itself you
To keep me out cold.
Believe me, I will not win.
Healing hurts worse than suffering in sin,
And more terrifying than cowering
beneath the darkness within.
I'm sorry, dear one
For the wounds
The anger.
The darkness.
The abuse.
For every moment you cry out for peace
And I make war.
For every night you go to bed aching
In body, mind, and soul,
And I give you more hatred than you ever deserved.
I'm sorry I can't love you,
that I never did in days behind,
And that I never will,
Because of the hidden poison in my mind.

***

ABOUT THE POEM
"Though part of me is dark
And full of blame for each permanent mark,
There is a small girl inside
Whose childhood was stolen, and her innocence died.
She is the one who really suffers here,
For I am the subject of all her fear."

POWER OF IMAGINATION

These words in rhythm and rhyme
Are beautified by aging and time.
Though they portray suffering in a bearably painful way,
Truth is far darker than I dare say.
Every word here written is desperately true,
But they are shadows, reality's mere hue.
You see, I must write color into a world of neutrality
I must find joy when racked with brutality.
I must see beauty in pain,
Else I have no strength to remain.
If you can turn your suffering into a masterpiece,

Someday you will find inner peace.
No injury can keep you down
If you can turn around every frown.
All the prisoners who survive captivity
Learn to let their souls find activity.
The invisible part of us holds the most life
After our bodies decay from lethal strife.
Any work of art
Is the product of someone's aching heart.
You must know loneliness to feel loved by someone.
You will only be free once many dark battles, you've won.
The pain is necessary for happiness,
We simply must pass the test.
So many do not make it out
Because they give in to fear and doubt.
Take my words, traveler,
Don't look at this with an attitude cavalier.
No disease is wholly escapable
To suffer like this, everyone is capable.
But, keep your head up.
Though you may be passed the bitter cup,
Gold is tested in fire,
And warriors are made in situations dire.
Turn these hard days into glorious expeditions.
Imagination makes bearable all conditions.

***

ABOUT THE POEM
"Some people say I have talent,
But to me it is the only way I can appear gallant.
The storms of life can be so fierce,
But in verse is my escape from the dagger's pierce."

ABOUT ELEANOR
As a child, Eleanor developed a love for writing of all kinds. In discovering Dr. Suess, she was encouraged to take up her own endeavors at writing, but it wasn't until she suffered from severe mental health issues as a pre-teen and teen that she really dedicated much time to it. Without a true friend to depend on, verse became her sole source of consolation and survival. Now she has discovered a true love and appreciation for poetry, and frequently express not only her dark thoughts in verse, but also love, joy, nature. One day, she hopes, this hobby will become a career.

Poetry by Carl Papa Palmer

CONFRONTING THE ENEMY

What reason do you have to steal into my marriage,
confiscate my husband with your morbid romance,
of all men why did you choose my man, Whore?

Why bring yourself into our house, disrupt our life,
arrive unexpected, unasked, unwanted, unwarranted,
can't you realize what you're doing to us, Heathen?

Why wrangle his thoughts, mangle his memories,
infiltrate his mind, defeat dreams, doom his future,
obscure his consciousness, confuse reality, Harlot?

Why not come out, face me, show me who are you,
what are you calling yourself today, you Sick Bitch,
or is your name still Alzheimer's, Senility or Dementia?

ABOUT THE POEM
*"When a member of the family is affected, the whole family is
affected, especially the spouse."*

ABOUT CARL
Carl is retired from the military and Federal Aviation Administration
(FAA), enjoying life as "Papa" to his grand descendants, and being a
Franciscan Hospice volunteer.

Poetry by Sandra Kacher

OIZYS

Seventy now,
hating these jellied upper arms
jiggling on the open window frame
of a rusted Chevrolet.

As I bump along
an aimless flinty road,
memories surface
from a dark heart-cave—

> *not a swimmer,*
> *clumsy, self-banished,*
> *shivering on the wet shoreline*

> *I cull myself from a cluster*
> *of dancers' twirling skirts,*
> *straightlaced among the ruffles*

> *covetous, wistful*
> *longing for my lost rhythm*
> *exiled from my home planet*

my arms are beautiful.
I have missed my life.

ABOUT THE POEM
"This poem reflects the depression I've worked with since adolescence."

ABOUT SANDRA
Sandra's profession was psychotherapy and, like many therapists, anxiety and depression were her companions. Her collection poetry is titled *First Confession*, and reflects this depression.

Poetry by Patrick G. Hughes
(PGH - THE NEO-REVSOLUTIONIST)

HAUNTED SUN / WINTER'S SON

Complicated thoughts intrude my unsettled mind
Infuriating my logic;
Controlling all words and each action,
They develop a persona

- An imitation of a man, who dwells in the distance.

And an angry word infiltrates an ordinary conversation
Expecting to be heard,
The temper'd voice will rise.
It shatters that common moment,

- I smell this man's voice in those cold moments of despair

> So, shut the windows
> Close the curtains and blinds
> Lock the doors
> Hideaway from lights and time
> And houl your whisht

> Speak of nothing, to no-one!

> Compress those thoughts
> As loud as prop guns
> Weighted now - like the Winter's Sun

An unprovoked reflex shocks, and shocks a loved one
A fist thumps an arm chair
Then the finger will point
It disturbs and it is remember'd

- The deceitful man returns, disguising himself in me

A regretful smile - though brief - captures yet another moment
Conversation - less frustration
And gesture - less provocation
Allows comfort; normality will pause: retreat!

- I banish this man, his reflexes and stench

So, empty the cupboards
Turn off images and sounds
Cover up the mirrors
Deny clowns, on Holy grounds
And houl your whisht.

Speak of nothing, to no-one
Control legacy emotions
Never dusted or done
Weighted now - like the Winter's Sun,

Life matters inhabit the daily routines
With general topics discussed
Between Television, work and upstairs vigils -
Normality remembers us
And, it is cautiously embraced

- I know this man implodes with prepossessed angst

Happiness escapes from worry, from depression.
A loved one becomes content
As I subtract and differentiate.
A skeletal future of side-tracks and back-roads is evident.

- This man of animosity; now - fading into my past

So, put the hate on,
Shelter from the coul,
Remove plugs from sockets.
Stuff the supermarket fowl
And, houl your whisht

Speak of nothing, to no-one!

Conceal the opinions
Hard fought and won,
Weighted now - like the Winter's Sun

Ambitious self-beliefs perpetrate my vision
But, inaccuracy is what I feel.
What I know and what I am sure of is remote
Yet, I am still offered love, tolerance and acceptance

- The contemptuous facade of man is angry to be ignored

I engage with my critics, my accusers
But, their voices are too low,
Their gestures, unrecognisable
Therefore, I am concealed,
within past, without future

- This man has made me Jeckyl to his Hyde

        So, press on the Super Sur
        Throw coats over the bed,
        Light the battery candles
        Glue St Martin's body to his head
        And, houl your whisht

            Speak of nothing, to no-one!

        Condemn the deeds
        Of all Fathers and Sons,
        Weighted now - like the Winter's Sun

ABOUT THE POEM
"This Dual-Poem, parallel to each other, represents my relationship with my late step-father who was mentally, physically and emotionally abusive towards me - and, how years of oppression and ridicule throughout our fractured relationship caused me to somehow inherit his mannerisms and temperament"

SOUL IMAGE: THE PROPHETIC

I dare not sleep
For, in sleep, I dream
And, in dreaming, I dream
Of not waking;
A surface fear, elevated
By a conflicting sickness and desire
Within my -
Semi-Self-Consciousness,
To accept such scenario and outcome
So, I dare not dream
For, to dream, I must sleep
And,
I am afraid of sleep's arrival.

ABOUT THE POEM
"This poem deals with insomnia and the fears, anxieties and panic-attacks that occur before, in between and after sleep."

THE PAYMENT OF DEPTHS

1. BARGAINING FOR MUTUAL BENEFIT
2. YOUR HEART'S NOT YOUR WEALTH

Furthermore - and study,

They have been strategically calculated
In threading the aesthetic boards
Over the anatomised bridges
That they have burnt,

Whilst He has climbed
The vertical and horizontal ladders
Then dived
Into the deep-end of the

Shallows -
To swim with sleeping Sharks

       He is guilty when making plans
       He is sad when catching that smile,
       Doubtful when contemplating

       Then,
       Disoriented for a while -

And She has pushed
The increasingly burdened boulders
And pebbles
Up and over Molehill Mountains

       She is angry when with laughter
       She is despaired when left alone,
       Nervous when in companionship

       And,
       In pretend comfort zones -

And, here am I,

I am confused by the certainties
I am afraid of fear itself,
Avoiding all that's inevitable

Because,
Our health is Not our wealth.

And I have stretched and reached
For shooting stars,
With my head peaking through
The silver-lined #9 clouds.

Furthermore - and document,

They have had their clipped feathered Wings
Scorched by the low Winter sun
As they each stood on shoulders,
Upon soap-box,
On top of pedestals,

Whilst He has stood behind
Lectured (Clerical and Academic) pulpits
Preaching to the Avant-Garde converted
And to the easily perverted subverted,

> He is frustrated with conversations
> He is bemused by pose and stance,
> Distraught by the political

> Then,
> Strutting off from the dance -

As She has walked barefoot
On ancient ghostly mythic footprints,
In Twilight -
Over city swamps and rural quicksands,

> She is happiest under rain clouds
> She is down when not in shade,
> Head lowered for invisibility

> And,
> Dissolving before the fade -

And, here am I,

> I am everything with nothing
> I am stuck up on the shelf,
> Never content or satisfied

> Because,
> Our health is Not our wealth.

And, I have used pen, plectrum and Brush
To dig my burial hole
For my cremated remnants
To be ritualistically buried,
Amalgamated with the cum-stained Earth

Furthermore - and index,

They have sat upon and straddled the Fences
Then ignoring borders and boundaries,
Limitations and restrictions,
They have stood on each of the greener Sides,

Whilst He has rebelliously whispered
Song and spoken word truths
As he rocked and rolled
the boat that he rowed -
Down white water pagan streams
And still silent rivers,

> He is drowning in mediocrity
> He is battling internal voices,
> Shouting into the void

> Then,
> Regretting decisions and choices -

As She has stared at the Abacus,
Counting blessings and Magpies
On her crossed fingers,
With one hand clapping,
And with an arm tied behind her back,

> She is lethargic when there's joy
> She is asleep to pass the time,
> Dreaming hard into nightmares

And,
Being punished for lesser crimes -

And, here am I,

I am strategic when I'm fatigued
I am less confident when not myself,
Manipulating the outcomes

Because
Our health is Not our wealth.

And, I have been rubbed up the right way,
And, I have ran my back up to
And banged my head against
The real and illusioned red brick peace Walls.

Furthermore - and archive,

They have been (verbally and physically)
Stabbed in front of their backs,
By the viral-tainted,
Who smiled,
When palming their biting hands
And when accepting their sweated Embraces,

Whilst He has seen Jesus in dead men's Eyes
And on blood-stained earth,
He has cried
The salted tears for exiled angels,

He is as high as Shangri-la
He is as low as the bass notes,
Resonating against bones
And,
Disturbing the counting of votes -

And She has manipulated her ways
Through windows -
When front and backs doors were Slammed,
Against her two-faces,
With access to entrances and exits
Denied to the multiples of She,

She is absent without leaving
She is in Purgatory's jail.
Unsure of the class and status

And,
Questioning how morality fails -

And, here am I,

I am lost in the boundaries.
I fracture ceramic hearts and delph.
Regurgitating the guilt

Because,
Our health is NOT our wealth!

And, I have loved too hard
And lusted too easy,
Undercover on duvet days
And under the covers of
Made and unmade beds -
Beside demon-lover ghosts...
I am Remembering to forget.

Furthermore - and witness,

They have danced the fire,
Within the flames,
In a three-steps forward,
Two-steps back
Pursuit of life and other strange encounters,

And, here We are,

We stand when all are seated.
We are a multitude of selfs.
Unified but not attached

Because,
Our health is NOT our wealth!

And, we have shakin' that blue-tale dog
As it slept and as it lied,
And we tried to steal back
Our fat-stained bones -

Before being devoured,
By the Mongrel's blackness.

    As pilgrims, we hear its sermon

    Claiming,
    Our health is NOT our wealth!

ABOUT THE POEM
"This dual poem deals with social-anxiety and paranoia when we all feel the need to compare ourselves to others, to covet what others have; to believe that they have more than us, that they are elevated higher than us in class, education, employment, success etc. The truth is that 'everyone' is trying to make it, on a daily basis, through many obstacles and hurdles and that we all should recognise this! In essence, we should all learn how to read the room and be aware of each other's possible troubles and struggles."

ABOUT PATRICK
Patrick suffered from bi-polar: depression and nervous debilities along with suicidal tendencies, panic attacks, and addictions. He is a published poet certified in Teaching Adult Learners. He is also an aspirational novelist and award-winning short prose writer certified in Entrepreneurship Skills; a recipient of (Go For It) N.I Business Start Programme; a collaborative and recording songwriter, certified in delivering project management for community arts; and a produced playwright and internationally experienced director holding BA Hons Degrees in English & Drama (Including Film & Psychology Studies) and MA Degree in English & Interdisciplinary Arts. He is now looking to help himself and others through his poetry.
W: www.Theneo-revsolutionist.com

Poetry by Simon Drake

MONSTER (My Story)

Oh how I despise you
Do you know I wished you dead
I wanted you to suffer mercilessly
For everything you did and said

Decades, haven't dulled my anger
My venom is still as potent
My hatred burns like molten lava
I was treated like a rodent

I will never ever forgive you
Disguised pretty and polite
An inability for any empathy
Even your smile was filled with spite

I remembered every time you hurt me
All bad deeds were filed
Your poison was my nourishment
You breastfed me as a child

The know it all's, knew nothing
Yeah but she's still your mother you know
You don't know what she went through
I think you should let this go

Punched in the face
I was kicked on the floor
By your wonderful boyfriend
You knew the score

If only people could have seen you
For the monster that you are
You should of been held accountable
For my lifetime's worth of scars

Told I was never wanted
You didn't deserve me as your son
From my lips you will never hear
Me ever call you Mum

So desperate to get back at you
Wanting to even up the score
I have done so, by finally letting go
I don't hate you any more!

RECONNECT

Tears are words yet to be written
My pain a verse in this muse
Recovery shall be my new mantra
It works, it might work for you

Stories swim in emotion
One event can take precedence
On replay, ten times a day
Hurt with no sight in end

Voices screaming for justice
Pounding inside of your head
Are they wrong, you stopped listening
Your feelings think that you're dead

Don't waste time looking for villains
Pointing fingers in anger or shame
Healing begins if you let go of things
Focus on love and not who's to blame

Reconnect your mind and body
To Jump start, plug into the soul
In the light of the sun you are now one
At last again you feel whole

MASK

Every single day I am crying
You only ever see my smile
Every day I pickup my pieces
Tears in single file

I am riddled with regret
I mourn children I've never had
Even though he's still alive
I mourn the loss of my Dad

I wish I'd made different choices
I wish I was brave enough to see
I'm stuck, I can't take this mask off
It's now a part of me

I live in a world of utter darkness
Not wanting you to know
Presenting as confident and happy
A facade, it's just a show

I've been wearing this since childhood
A prison with me under lock and key
If I took it off in front of the mirror
Would a child stare back at me

DROWNING IN SADNESS

Silence my friend and protector
Consumed with grief, heartache and loss
At home in the shadow of darkness
Content to just sit here and watch

No one knows what I'm truly feeling
Pain sets fire to hope every day
Continuously drowning in sadness
I could but I won't walk away

A recording that's become a defence mechanism
If I'm stuck and don't know what to say
I'm fine, don't worry about me
The lie that continues to play

Childhood doesn't prepare you for adulthood
Lessons you needed to survive
Love, disappointment and loneliness
How darkness is able to thrive

I've had to find my own way in life
Whispers of uncertainty filled my mind
Never sure what I should be searching for
In places so bitter, harsh and unkind

ABOUT THE POEMS
"Poetry has been a huge form of personal therapy for me, being able to tap into emotions and express my inner feelings through writing has been a wonderful healthy release."

ABOUT SIMON
Simon is a Gestalt counsellor, spoken word performer, published poet and martial artist. Having a years worth of grief Counselling on the NHS changed the direction of Simon's life putting him on a path of hope and healing. After five years of studying, he is now able to help those that need support and encouragement the most.

Poetry by Kesia Burdett

MESSAGES NEVER SENT

Do you know when you're struggling,
And feeling alone,
And you so badly want to tell someone,
So you pick up your phone?
You type out a message,
And get it all out,
You desperately want help,
You could scream it out loud.
But you sit there in silence,
And backspace the message,
Because you're so afraid of hurting,
And you just want to forget this.
You can't even speak,
Or say it out loud,
But you wish someone could hear you,
Without making a sound.
Without having to explain,
Without having to feel,
They just understand,
And know that your pain is real.
But I always backspace the message,
Because if I put it all down,
I realize I'm suffering,
And I want to break down.
And so I remain silent,
Hoping someone will hear me,
Because the pain is too deep,
And I cannot think clearly.
A cry for help but saying nothing at all,
Until the pain is overwhelming,
Until I can't anymore.
But I firmly believe that these words unspoken,
Nourish the growth that comes when the heart feels broken
We are not alone,
We are not to feel ashamed,
Because when our words are spoken, is when the world will change.
Be the light,
Have some faith,
Change the world
With every brave step you take.

The light is not gone, but merely slightly dim
So light that fire that burns so beautifully within.
All is not lost,
We have to fight on,
And show those who are struggling the great things that will come.

ABOUT THE POEM
"'Messages Never Sent' paints a picture of those quiet, tough moments when words fail us. It's about that text you type out but never send, the cry for help that's hard to share. It's a glimpse into the struggle of feeling alone and not knowing how to reach out. This poem is not just about suffering in silence; it's also a reminder that we all have felt this way, and we're not alone in it."

DISTRACT YOURSELF

Distract yourself,
Just a little more,
Just for one more hour,
It's okay to ignore.
All the intrusive thoughts,
And the stabbing pain,
You can deal with it tomorrow,
Or another day.
Don't even think about it,
Or talk at all,
It will hurt too much,
Just continue to ignore.
You can face it when you're stronger,
Doesn't have to be today,
Even when you're 90 years old,
And have lived with all the pain.
Don't waste your life,
It goes quicker than you think,
Embrace all that you are,
And remember why you are here,
And water the draught that exists around us
With your beautiful tears.

ABOUT THE POEM
"'Distract Yourself' was born from the days when I felt overwhelmed by my thoughts and emotions. It's about those times when facing our inner demons feels too raw, too real, so we tell ourselves, "Not today." This poem is a reminder that it's a journey we all go through.

I wanted to reach out to anyone who has felt the need to put off dealing with pain or mental challenges, to let them know they're not alone. It's a conversation with myself and with others, saying that it's okay to need time but also highlighting the importance of eventually facing what we fear."

THE GIRL YOU NEVER KNEW

Let me tell you about the girl who was labelled a slut,
The one whose father was never there when she was growing up.
Let me tell you about the girl who you claim seeks attention,
The girl who cried herself to sleep, wishing she had any sort of affection.
Let me tell you about the girl who struggles with self-esteem,
The girl who was never good enough, trying hard to people please.
Let me tell you about the girl who's struggling with her thoughts,
The one who you judge,
Knowing nothing at all.
Let me tell you about the girl who's struggling with her weight,
The one you tease to no lengths,
Until she starves to feel safe.
Let me tell you about the girl who tries so hard to fit in,
The one who's not thin or pretty enough,
Who feels bad in her own skin.
Let me tell you about the girl who longed for love's embrace,
The one who sought after connection, in every wrong place.
She's the girl who holds a mirror to society's face,
The one you scorn and ridicule, yet she shows incredible grace.
See, this girl you cast aside is stronger than you know,
If that girl is you, your extraordinary glow
Will lead you to love yourself, as you've needed long ago
And all the pain will clear your path; with grace, you'll undergo.
Those who judged you once will face reflections of their own,
Lost in shadows, haunted by the cruelty they've shown.
But in your heart, keep faith and grace, never feel alone,
Embrace your purpose, love yourself, let your true light be known.

ABOUT THE POEM
"'The Girl You Never Knew' speaks to the universal experience of feeling judged, misunderstood, and never quite good enough. Drawing from my own experiences, the poem tears away at labels and prejudices to reveal the resilient heart within. It paints a picture not just of one girl, but of anyone who has felt overlooked or underestimated by the world. Whether it's a struggle with self-

esteem, fitting in, or simply feeling good enough, this poem is a reflection of our shared human journey. It's a call to kindness and an affirmation of the strength and extraordinary glow that exists within us, even when others fail to see it."

ABOUT KESIA
Kesia writes poems that resonate with the heart and soul, and delves into personal experiences and the shared human condition - focusing particularly on mental health struggles. Writing has been her therapy, her passion, and her way of reaching out to others, and through poetry, she attempts to understand, connect, and heal.
Instagram: @becomingmeinafrica
Instagram: @kesiabee

Poetry by Charly White

MESS

My body sighs out - yes
as I stop, sit down and rest
my self-conscious fights back, grows
feeling weak and insecure
my self-image - worried, vain
you'll lose everything you've gained
so my mind screams back NO - get back up, push forward, GO!
but my body resists
once more
and it's she,
who has never
lied to me
before

ABOUT THE POEM
"Battling with guilt, judgments and self-depreciation for not constantly pushing myself to my limits. I end this poem by choosing to listen to my body over my mind, knowing how deceiving my own thoughts can be."

FUEL

I have allowed food
to fuel
a toxic mind
rather than
a healthy heart
and I'm unsure
how
to press
undo

ABOUT THE POEM
"An acknowledgment of my unhealthy relationship with food and how I have created patterns / thought processes that strengthen it, rather than fighting against it and working towards being healthier in body and mind."

THE MENTAL HEALTH WARD

'Hello, Gran, how are you today?'
'Fine' she'd respond and turn her face away
she knew who I was but had nothing to say
no desire to engage, no desire to play
she'd given up on words, what good were they now?
already failed her in attempts
to convince us of how
TO HELP
break her out of the prison she was kept
spun tales of her torture, whilst she pleaded and wept

~

but then 5pm struck, so we got up to leave
with a pitiful attempt to quickly wrap up the grief
making sure she was safe
in the space she was held
the small cosy room,
her own mind - where she fell
'Bye gran, I love you. I'll see you tomorrow'.
'Don't bother' she'd spit back
and I left
drowned in sorrow

ABOUT THE POEM
"A narrative of a harrowing time in my life, visiting my gran in hospital as she tried to survive with dementia during the last years of her life. There was so much distress, bitterness, resentment and guilt wrapped up in this time. As helpless as we all felt, each day we kept going just the same, doing only what we could do and swallowing the pain that came with it."

THE DARKNESS

Yes, I knew
you were coming
I could feel it
in my spine
I had scheduled
your arrival
yes, I knew
you're right on time

but I'm not here
to start a battle
to let you drain me
of my life
for I know
if I keep waiting
that the dawn
will soon arrive

ABOUT THE POEM
"An acknowledgment of the dark times and difficult periods in life that are inevitable and recurring. Waiting for its arrival and being sure of its departure creates a sense of strength in my ability to see it through and overcome it, whatever it may be this time."

CARRYING SMILES

When will it finally
sink in
that people notice
how I carry
myself, not
how I carry
my weight
and I would much rather
carry myself
with a smile
than to crush myself
with this weight

ABOUT THE POEM
"An acknowledgment of how dangerous my own thoughts and self-image can be, keeping me stuck in the realms of self-harming habits and behaviours. I try to adopt a perspective that disproves my own thoughts and shows a reality where my toxic behaviours make less sense, to hopefully inspire some positive behaviour changes."

ABOUT CHARLY
Charly is a 26 year-old writer from South Wales, in the UK. She will be publishing her first poetry collection in January 2024. Her writing focuses on mindfulness, nature and mental health, exposing the most raw and difficult moments in life alongside the most magical. She sees writing as a therapy; it has helped her through so many challenging periods of her life and she hopes that in sharing her

words, they are able to provide the same comfort and hope for her readers.
Social media: @charlyannwhite
The Poetry Garden: @the.poetrygarden

Poetry by Duane Anderson

WHERE DID MY LIFE GO?

What am I doing,
what am I not doing?
I guess I must pay attention in order
to know what is happening in my life.

Why am I wearing nothing one day,
the day when I was born,
and on another day, a suit and tie,
the day of my funeral.

What was I wearing the days in between,
and where did all the days go,
but I guess it is too late to question my life
after I have departed this earth.

Go ahead,
attend my funeral if you know me.
Maybe you know what went right
and wrong in my life.

ABOUT THE POEM
"Sometimes I look back at my life, and ask myself did I live a good life, and if there is any reason to keep on living. Will it be worth it, but as always, I get through moments like this."

THE END OF LIFE

No one listened to the words I spoke
or heard the words that did not
leave my throat.

The air was still,
there was no movement
as people sat in their chairs.

Tears flowed down cheeks,
silently, of those nearby.
No one would tell me

what was going on.
No one would tell me that
I was no longer alive.

ABOUT THE POEM
"I have been very shy my entire life, never one to talk very much. It is very hurtful, and I at times feel like I am living in a world doing just fine without me. Again, all alone by myself."

WALKING IN THE WILDERNESS

I looked into the mirror
hoping to find myself,
but it only laughed at me,
telling me I was looking
in the wrong place.

I looked again,
but it kept laughing.
I was puzzled,
it was not,
telling me to go elsewhere.

I was nowhere to be found,
and moved to another room in the house,
drawing a picture of myself on the wall,
and there I was, finding
my place in the world.

ABOUT THE POEM
"I sometimes think about my life, is it worth continuing, then I find out that it is, writing poems saves me."

ABOUT DUANE
Duane currently lives in Nebraska, USA. He has had poems published in *Fine Lines, Cholla Needles, Tipton Poetry Journal*, and several other publications. He is the author of *On the Corner of Walk and Don't Walk, The Blood Drives: One Pint Down*, and *Conquer the Mountains*.

Poetry by Sanda Ristić Stojanović

WHAT WE ARE GOING TO DO IN THE FUTURE

We will sit on the shore,
the sea will turn her heart into us,
the shores will draw everything
the shapes of our anxiety, our joy.

We will sit on the shore,
reality will be uttering this century
loud enough to be heard by
the Moon and
doppelgängers of our anxiety,
and doppelgängers of our longing.

We will sit on the shore,
words will resemble the Moon,
words will have the identity card of the Sun,
words will weigh the body contours and
meaning of the word star.

We will sit on the shore
the sea will identify herself with our clairvoyance,
the high and low tides will emulate our glares,
the roar of our inner Moon,
our mirrors that have the depth of other people's words.

We will sit on the shore,
The Moon and the Sun will have the costumes of our time,
the heavens and the earth will have our hands and
will touch the future of song
and the future of the spoken.

We will sit on the shore,
and that of the coast of time
where our hours will dance like
the human reflection of the precious metal of reality.

We will sit on the shore,
two, three, poets and
two, three, poetesses will be
the catharsis of a bonfire of time.

We will sit on the shore,
the sparks of time will provoke
the hands of reality to touch our poems.

THE SOLDIER WHO REMAINED ON THE BATTLEFIELD

The murmur of death enters into his heart,
That's where the world lays
Germinated through the skull of the Sun.

The wind describes him as
The essence of the Sun that lays
Riddled,
Many times with sorrow of,
All areas of duration.

The sadness of autumn closes his eyes,
It radiates the collapse of death,
In one lament of
All waiting mothers for
The soldiers' return.

ABOUT THE POEMS
During the NATO bombing of Serbia and Belgrade in 1999, with my colleagues Biljana and Dragica, I carried books from the bookstore to the tables in front of the bookstore, because there was neither electricity nor water in the street. At that time, I was an editor at the Beletra publishing house (1998-2000), I was 25 years old, I had an office on the other side of town. When the bombing started in 1999, I moved to a bookstore in the very centre of the city and sold books in front of the bookstore to earn wages. Biljana, Dragica and I gave 2–3 interviews for various journalistic teams from around the world who were constantly passing through that main street (Knez Mihailova). A Spanish press team took a picture of us and published that picture in a Spanish daily newspaper. It was the beginning of May 1999, an air danger was announced over Belgrade. I remember the conversation between Biljana and me:
Biljana – And what if we die?
Me - We will not die
Biljana - Are you sure?
Me – Yes, I am sure."

Dedicated to Biljana N. (1972 – 2009, car accident)

ABOUT SANDA

Sanda is a poet and aesthetic. Born in Belgrade, she graduated in philosophy at the Belgrade Faculty of Philosophy. She is the author of 15 poetry books, and one of four authors in the joint collection of poems *From the Shadow of the Verse* (Gramatik, 2012). Her poems and short stories were published in numerous collections of contemporary literature, and in several anthologies of the poetry of the twenty-first century. She is a member of the Serbian Literary Society, the Association of Serbian Writers, and the Aesthetic Society of Serbia.

Poetry by Frances Gaudiano

SPRING LAMB

It was a late lamb,
Spindly legs staggering after the ewe.
Too weak to bleat.
Not a nursery rhyme lamb:
White, fluffy and beribboned.
This one was drab,
Muddy.

We too, have stumbled into brackish puddles,
Yearning to be washed clean
Gentle rain,
Making us new again.
But we are grey,
Mottled by the dirt of years,
Scrambling after sustenance,
Waiting for the sun.

A VERY SMALL PERSON

I've killed the cockroaches for you.
The dogs have chased the rats away.
All the door are locked.

You are safe.

Come sit beside me,
 my arm around your shoulders,
I'll hold you close.

The blankets tented over us,
We'll use a torch to read
stories in the darkness.

Some of these tales will be true,
others make-believe;
I wrote them all for you.

Time has taught me a thing or two.
I know how to protect you now.

I'm sorry it's taken so long.

CRY ME AN OCEAN

You can cry underwater
No one notices
A few more drops in the sea.
Ask the sea turtles
With their litres of salt tears.

Make the world your ocean.
Fill it with your sadness,
Then watch the tide take it all away.
Step away clean.

Go to a new beach.
Dig deep, burying eggs of hope.
Maybe this time
Something beautiful will hatch.

ABOUT THE POEMS
*"I battled eating disorders and depression for a large part of my life.
There are still some scary days but things are pretty good now. I
think my poems are beginning to reflect that you can fall in the black
pit but there is a way out, eventually."*

ABOUT FRANCES
Frances lives in Cornwall, England. She is a veterinary nurse by day,
and a writer in all her spare moments. Her novel *The Listener* was
published in 2021, and its sequel is due out later this year. She has
also had poetry and short stories appear in a variety of online and
print journals, and she is the author of a textbook on Veterinary
Dermatology.

Tania Lowerson's story

Four walls all around me
Padded and white
When I scream no one hears me
Is it day or is it night.

My food is pushed through a flap in the door,
But how can I eat when my head feels sore.
An end to this madness an end to it all.

I sit alone in the corner banging my head against the wall.

I wasn't sure when this disease started, but something was growing inside my mother. It changed her personality. One day she would be the loving, caring mother the next day a MONSTER - verbal abuse, physical abuse, blaming: "You are the devils child, you will never amount to anything." The locks on the bedroom door, the fear and anxiety every day of trying to gauge which mother was picking me up from infant school.

I dreamt of suicide at eight years old and started to drink bath cleaner in the hope it would kill me. Years later I would take several overdoses. I tried running away too, to be found by my father, who was oblivious to what my mother was doing. I wanted that family up the street - who were always smiling and happy, not pretending when we had visitors at the door.

I was screaming inside, trapped in my bedroom - which was my sanctuary. Here I could not be blamed for everything. "Wait till your father comes home," she would spit through gritted teeth - it was a teddy bear, stuffing strewn around the floor.

It was not always me, it was my sister too, but I protected her - I did not like to see her getting hit with my fathers belt, so I would say it was me. I would get the belts for her. I did not care any more, I hardened myself. Then one day, as my father was taking his belt off, he looked at me and said: "It's not always you is it?" That was when he first realised something was wrong.

My mother had two admissions into mental health hospitals throughout her life. Mental illness broke our family up. Years spent in counselling, suffering depression, anxiety and P.T.S.D. We all screamed for help years ago, but help was not forthcoming unless she was a danger to herself or to others. At the moment my mum remains stable - as long as she takes her medication. My mother divorced my father, she now lives alone.

I have now worked in Mental Health for 15 years, and through my experiences I was able to help others that were in crisis; to sit and listen to their stories, to help heal others.

Poetry by Kai Amber

FRESH SCENT

Heavy is the grime,
that depression leaves over time,
but poems cause hopes renewal,
and ease doubts more than a few,
to clean away all the fears and their resent,
to leave the soul with a fresh scent.

Damn, Are You Sedated?

They all thought I was on drugs,
when I was just plagued with a brain full of bugs.
Every word that destroys got deployed,
to break me down and push me to the void.
So heavily weighted,
brains thinking, 'Damn, are you sedated?'

Now the meds are starting to flow,
and glimmers of me are starting to show.
Trying to bring it back from the brink ,
and pray this time I won't sink.

ABOUT KAI
Kai is a 38 year-old AFAB non-binary former customer service
representative turned poet and story writer. Kai struggles with
mental health, but write poems to work through their mental issues,
and to convince themself, and others, to persist and to not give up.
Poetizer: @Kai Amber

Poetry by Melanie Kerr

DEMENTIA

She was mugged
Not in broad daylight
Not watched
By the unblinking eye
Of a CTV camera
No grainy pictures
Of unidentifiable yobs
Snatching a handbag
And pushing her to knees
Leaving her trembling

She was mugged
Not on a crowded street
Where people pretend
It's not their business
And hide behind
Carrier bags and trolleys
And only after it's safe
Do they reach out
To help her back to her feet
Leaving her shaken

She was mugged
In the safety of her own home
No balled up fists
Or snarling threats
Just the silent destruction
Of neurons and pathways
In the brain
The relentless dismantling
Of memories and thoughts
Leaving her confused

Now she sits in a nursing home
Folded in a red chair
Frantically picking
At a blanket that covers
Her knees
Blue clouded eyes
Searching for familiar landmarks

The lines erased
Between then and now
Leaving her adrift

ABOUT THE POEM
"My mother-in-law suffered from vascular dementia and spent the last ten years of her life in a nursing home. For her is was like a sudden switching off the lights, nothing slow or gradual. My husband and I used to visit her regularly but she didn't recognize us. It broke my heart that my husband used to have this one-sided conversation, him asking the questions and answering on her behalf."

ABOUT MELANIE
Melanie has recently retired from teaching. She and her husband live in Inverness, Scotland. Melanie has been writing poetry, short stories and devotionals for a number of years. She has self-published two collections of poetry, *Wider Than the Corners of This World* and *A Thousand Dulux Shades of Life*. She plans to publish a third book of poetry later on in the year. Melanie is currently studying part-time at the University of Highlands and Islands. If things go according to plan, she should receive a BA in Creative Writing when she is 70 years old.

Poetry by Tayane De Oliveira

POWERLESS - I CRY FOR HELP

Tied into my mind
I must know what's wrong.
Why do I feel such pain?
When I am alright in the doctor's eyes

I feel like bursting into tears.
Since it hurts.
The pain in my guts
Makes my head explode,
As well as my body shake.
My insides burn me from within.
As if they were trying to say something.
Nonetheless, you think it's just a headache.
From a hangover from something I might have just taken.

Please just break my bones.
So I can be taken away
Without being questioned.
Perhaps then I won't feel this pain.
This one comes from within.
And it can't be easily found.

What if I scream? but this time, not only on the inside.
Why do I know that if I do so,
No one will care?
Regardless of what I say,
As long as I look okay.

I was told I was well.
Can that be true?
I know I need help.
Still, how will I get it?
If no one cares to believe me and mental health is taboo.

ABOUT THE POEM
"'Powerless - A Cry for Help' emerges from the depths of an invisible battle that so many face in solitude. It springs forth from the heartache of seeking understanding amidst a world that struggles to perceive the pain etched within. The poem invites, with its simplicity, the uninitiated to explore the uncharted territories of empathy and

the power of belief – a belief in the legitimacy of the battles fought within."

ABOUT TAYANE
Tay was born in Brazil and is now residing in Germany. The written word has become her vessel to navigate the depths of human emotions. She finds herself drawn to the shadows and the melancholic corners of the heart, unveiling the layers that define consciousness. She is fascinated by the intricate complexities that emotions bring to life and often aims to show them through the heaviest of sorrows. It's her aspiration that her words possess the ability to transcend the pages, transporting readers to realms of profound introspection so that they can dive into the core of their own emotions and thoughts, finding resonance and connection. Just as she has been transformed by her writing journey, she hopes that others can also embark on a path of self-discovery through the emotions she lay bare on the page.

Poetry by Angus Shoor Caan

DIVE FOR YOUR MEMORY

I look on aghast as you dive for your memory
Delve deep for words once within your vocabulary
The struggle etches lines into your beautiful face
Bewilderment reigns, of your smile there's no trace.

I never once dreamt you'd be stuck for a word
Your bright conversation the very song of a bird
Now muted, replaced with both puzzle and pain
Not a hint of response to the sound of your name.

Selfishly, you've come out of it best in a sense
I say this with sadness but truly in your defence
There's grief for my loss although you're still alive
Without self awareness, without purpose or drive.

I talk to you constantly, you simply stare at your feet
While friends and neighbours ask for you in the street
They don't see my tears, my apathetic solemnity
See me weep as I watch you dive for your memory.

ABOUT THE POEM
"A few years ago I witnessed my friend's memory skills rapidly decline, taking her physical health to task alongside it. I felt compelled to put my own thoughts and feelings down on paper and this is the result. The poem is part of a collection made use of by the Alzheimer's Society in a brochure to accompany their Christmas Carol Service in London."

ABOUT ANGUS
Angus is an author, poet, essayist and performance artist.

Poetry by Chloe Lauren Smith

HIJACK

The first time, well you never forget your first time. When you disappear behind the line, of reality. 100 thousand feet up, defying gravity. Terrified. The ground rules do not apply.

And all the security checks were taken, emergency landing card, visual demonstration. But no one knew who was inside, no one knew the turbulent ride.

To the outside eye none could be suspected - passengers and crew, no single threat detected. So first came shock, then instant denial. When the terrorist stood up with a gun in the aisle. Shouting in a tongue foreign to my land, with a smile on their face and a gun in the hand. This had been planned months in the making, 100 innocents or more, in this hostage situation. What paralysed me more was this was no chartered flight. But my departure from self in the middle of the night.

This was ground zero, my monument of sorrow. My mental plane hijacked, no hope for tomorrow. The terrorist kept shouting the language now mine, with the urging and bullying your running out of time. Sleepless nights, no appetite, yet tried so hard just to be. Crippled by anxiety, occupied by vacancy. I was already dying in this bottomless pit, being buried alive and not giving a shit. Something inside of me finally snapped. I found a flicker of my flame and planned my attack.

Armed with Jesus, therapy and my saris. I looked the terrorist in the face and decided my why. Why I wanted to live, why I wanted to fly. I speak for the ones under headstones that script "forever loved, forever be missed," but on my headstone it will say this: 'Did not negotiate with terrorists.'

SHADOW PLAY

She did not fear her shadow, for it was in the lack of light she found her most solid self.
No she was afraid to lose the infill and outlines of how sorrow had defined her, consumed her to hide her.
She was afraid of being seen, trace paper hearts in iron fists,

accustomed to the crushing of this. She came to understand early enough that there was no such thing as trust.
That people are for connection and objects to be used, translates as people for use and objects to connect,
Dopamine hits to replace emptiness.
She longed for the solid the raw and the real,
the razor blade helped her breathe gutting gills.
Coz the air that remained through longingly held breath may find its release and be repurposed yet.
Perhaps in a plant or the chlorophyll of trees, she could repurpose her life in a landscape of green.
She used to laugh and craft wisdom with words, to be misunderstood, frustrated, unheard.
So now she releases these words of wisdom in art, in the darkness with strangers unravels her heart.
Then plugs it with paper to slow down the bleed, retreat into shadows remaining unseen.
She is not angry or anxious or depressed, she is numb,
disillusioned by hope and what she's become.
She knows inside there is greatness, something to unlock,
but doesn't know how, and the clock ticks and tocks by, go the years the months and the days,
and she folds in on herself, 2D and grey.
She smiles and laughs, puppeteers the outside, but in the core of her being, on her island she cries.
Sends messages in bottles an SOS of her soul,
in attempt to be seen, in attempt to be whole.

ABOUT CHLOE
Chloe is a South West London spoken word artist and poet, graduating in 2011 from Winchester University with a degree in Creative Writing. She has worn many hats in her working career that have thematically centred around people, community and storytelling. She loves working with people from all walks of life, supporting those in addiction recovery, the young and marginalized, to the bereft. Finding the human spirits ability to overcome, adapt and transform to be the foundation of many a noteworthy story and the think-tank of courage. Chloe herself has suffered, at times acutely, from ill mental health, and her contributions to these works is derived from articulating her own experiences. *"It is a privilege and joy to be a constructive voice joining in the conversation of Mental Health, and I firmly believe that stories of lived experience can be someone else's survival guide."*

Poetry by Thomas William Oddie

HOPE

Hope and forgiveness
The things that I need
So I hope you forgive me
As my heart stops to bleed
It bleeds for memories
The love and your sole
Without you in this life
My world will never be whole
So I spin the pendant clockwise
To feel that you forgive
The end is not there yet for me
With so much life to live
My life will cease to mean a thing
Without someone my heart to lend
So I hope that you forgive me now
As I begin to mend
The memories I carry of you
Are edged in to my mind
So today I patiently wait for tomorrow
And the healing hand of time
This doesn't mean that I'll forget
Are whirlwind romance love
A piece of my heart
You'll always have
As you fly freely
In sky's above.

SHADOW AND THE STAR

Where to start
At the beginning
With the Shadow I suppose
Then I brilliant shooting star
The perfect petal rose
In my dreams we dance
We swing and we twirl
Then I wake and remember
You were to good for this world
Though my heart it yearns

For just one more day
I wish dreams were FOREVER
your embrace would make me stay
But forever is a wish
A wish that's just to far
So I'll see you every night
My love my shooting star.

IF I WAS YOU

If I was you
And you were me
Then I'd go blind
So you could see
See my life
And take the knife
To cut not once
But always twice
You see my brain
The mental pain
As life and time
Turn me insane
This invisible cage
And torn up rage
I show you now
With ink and page
The world spins round
I spiral down
Then hurt my self
Without a sound
The mental hole
Gets deeper and deeper
The come down stairs
Get steeper and steeper
Then all my thoughts
Will creep the creeper
Until the day I die.

NEVER ENDING DAY

There was still tomorrow
When I woke today
My sadness the same

As yesterday
My smile like yesterday
Has gone
I wish today
Tomorrow would come

ABOUT THE POEMS
"All the poems are about my drug and alcohol addiction, and my self-harming and bipolar depression."

Poetry by Tim Boardman

TEMPUS FUGIT

Having the
Grandmother
Clock
in the room
is disturbing

It means
Nothing
to me
apart from
Memories
of the chime

But it's not working

Transporting
The clock
in the car
From mum and dad's
Sounded
Like Pink Floyd
'Ticking away the moments
That make up a dull day'

As the car hits bumps

SCYTHE

There's nothing like
seeing your mother's
Tears
as you go to sleep
to hear her
Weeping
Leaving her
and us
in an emotional
Heap
last night

her voice breaking
Understanding
Her plight
Not wanting to be there
and not giving up
The Fight

'Nowhere is quite right
I don't want to end
My life here'
There's nowhere to hide
With people talking rubbish
And the hooded man
With a scythe
Peering in
From outside

ABOUT THE POEMS
"I've been a teacher for over twenty years teaching students with mental health issues - I still don't like 'mental health' as a term, there should be better words, more like: 'finding a way through', or 'finding a way to cope.' I have taught Art, English and Maths, also employability and life skills. Through this time I've always created art work, either through painting and collage or poetry. In the last three years we've had to find a way of dealing with my dad and his dementia, it's a terrible disease and had had a impact on my health and my families, the latest poems are my way of dealing with it."

Poetry by Rebecca Akrofie

THERE'S NOTHING ROMANTIC ABOUT, GHOSTS

There is nothing romantic about dying inside while you're still alive.
Depression is not like getting high
It is like being held underwater
It is like excruciating pain
Not the refreshing kind
It is not like being hit on the head and suddenly seeing clearly
It is just like being hit on the head.
It is not like being bitten by a spider, feeling ill and waking up with strange superpowers
It is like being bitten by a spider, feeling ill, and waking up strange
Waking up with just a head and some lungs
That's depression sometimes.
Not like an ache that gets better as the day goes on
More like an ache that leaves a permanent groove
That's the ghosts propping themselves up against your insides.
There's nothing romantic about dying inside, while you're still alive.

ABOUT REBECCA
Rebecca is a page poet from London. She has been reading on the London scene since 2018, at nights including Jawdance, Poetry LGBT, The Poetry Cafe, and Reference Point, as well as performing at The Albany Theatre. She is a regular of the London LGBTQ+ Centre poetry workshop. She is published in the United Press anthology *Home Thoughts* and *AZ Magazine*.

Poetry by Kenneth Yamikani Chiwaya

WHEN LONELINESS HITS

Everything looks unreal, exasperating and demeaning
All stances seem to be nauseated
When loneliness hits, even plants petrels with fluffy winds

The empty bowel seems to be full with adrenaline enzymes
That buries the needs for replica of the taste's buds
When loneliness hits, even the trees shake with cramped winds

The holding eternity seems to be piped down
Creating the holes inside the heart that discourage forty winks
When loneliness hits, even the shrubs dance the old songs of ebb
winds.

To be lonely sometimes it's not a choice
The suicidal ideations come but let it not be a solution
When loneliness hits, goof around and at least find someone to talk
to.

ABOUT THE POEM
*"The poem is trying to emphasize that yes, when you're depressed
you feel lonely, nothing seems to be working, and this might trigger
one to consider suicide, but it says that's not the best solution and
it's encouraging you to find someone you can trust and talk to about
what is eating you up."*

ABOUT KENNETH
Kenneth is Malawian based writer and poet, with a BSc in Water
Quality and Management. He started writing in 2015, when he was at
secondary school. Since then, he has been writing short stories and
poems, and has participated in several writers' groups and
associations. His first book *The Lost Pride* is in progress.
FB: @Kenneth Yamikani Chiwaya

Poetry by Prudence Massaria

ME, MYSELF AND I

In my aloneness Me, Myself and I
walk the beach
The Sand, color of wheat
Snow Capped Mountain Waves wash ashore
The Sky pure and intense, delphinium blue
Sun of Life, yellow-orange, shines rays
of light ONTO my heart to lead me from
the darkness of my soul
The darkness, encompassing

Me, Myself and I walk the beach from
dawn to dusk, dusk to dawn
A new day is born
Differently, the light shines THROUGH
my heart
I am led out of the darkness

Dawn has broken
Snow Capped Mountain Waves wash ashore
My footsteps imprinted on the sand I walk
with sure footing
Me, Myself and I

ABOUT THE POEM
"Perhaps it was being a "latch key kid" at the age of seven when the seed of emptiness was planted and germinated. I knew well what it meant to be alone and feel abandon emotionally. It was then I developed a relationship with sugar ... junk food - my escape from the loneliness of my home on return from school. Both parents worked to give me a better life and they did, however, there were negative consequences - emotional emptiness; my psychic trunk. Through years of therapy and love, my physic trunk is no longer vacant. I found wholeness in parenting, a career counselling heroin addicts afflicted with AIDS, writing, drawing and learning to play piano. The right side of the brain hemisphere united with the left together in unison ... music, the emotional language of my being. Forever grateful to all who are a part of my psychic trunk: Family, Friends, Patients, God the Universal Supreme."

Poetry by Karen Rowe

CHAMELEON FRIEND

At first I never questioned what you said,
You spoke it with such conviction and strength.
Gently approaching, and seductive as any caring lovers caress.
There in the lonely hours, when other
People had left, for the day, weeks or a lifetime.
You told me, it didn't matter. I didn't need them.
When it fact, you were pretending. You said you were
honest , but you kept changing colours, and what a colourful journey,
You took me on my chameleon friend.

Your voice that told me not to worry, you will cope
coloured with bright sun rays, then changed to black and altered to
tell me
I was the problem, I was stupid, and at fault.

Once in, you weaken me. Any slightest mistake or rebuke from a
person,
deepened my connection, to your altered perception.
Filling my head with such negative threads, comprehensive grey webs
That strangle and ensnare the feelings of, contentment and hope.
I can no longer feel their gold glow.

My behaviour changes, I withdraw, you are my only friend.
A bad one at that. You exhaust me with the stories you tell.
I am too vulnerable to challenge, that they are not facts.
After all, it's my own voice that's telling me that.
I am dimly aware that people speak to me, sending brief streams
of pale blue light, breaking through a dark canopy.
But I can't answer them honestly, You keep me too busy.

I sleep too much, too little, too often.
Despair fills my waking moments, and my dreams are never restful.
My life, outside my door, has become, the worst colour to me.
A bright, glaring pink that I just hate to see.
It's too intense, more input that my mind can take.
Please let me stay in, at least here, I don't need to fake.
That I like the colour and how it's great.

How sick i feel, and my heart starts to race.
I don't want to be here or at least be me.

When I walk, it's only in the country.
The hanging trees look the least odd to me.
Cutlery grips the skin with no food in place.
And when I drink enough, colourless liquid for four,
it fails to effect me anymore.

I realise I need help, I can't handle you by myself.
People don't seem to notice, but they only see me
You are well hidden. I have protected you, like
a shameful secret. As I altered within.
Your colours clash, with everything.

I get help, the white sweets from the doctor
make me feel sick, and really not like myself.
Even though, I am not really sure, what that means anymore.

I get help from a professional in a regional location.
But I can't get out the words, without using a mountain
Of soft paper. Over the course of weeks, the talk becomes more,
And the tears less. I am honest about
how I feel, which I haven't been since your conception,
gave me, battling through a sandstorm perception.
The sunlight rays, cutting through the blinds,
alters more than just the room, there brightness filtering my view.
I am grateful for the time now, even though at first I hated
the hands, that told me it was time.

My therapist made me laugh when a had a bad week.
I thank her, but she said, the hard work was mine,
But I feel, with her it was not a merely
employment, after education, but a true vocation.

Paper held dark ink diagrams which showed how insecure feelings,
developed when young, were being amplified, by you
nurturing all the negatives, to give you power.
The adapting thoughts effected my behaviour, into a self destructive
course.
I can control my reaction to lessen your force.

I realise I had surrounded myself
With people who reinforced that I was likeable, but I failed to see,
That one genuine friend is worth an infinite number
Of those who pretend. Only around when it benefits them.
Those who only take, which I kept fuelling, with the efforts I made.
I tolerated what I never should had accepted, In a desperate attempt

to never be alone with you. They were my holy water, against your
vampire soul.

It's hard not to take it personally, when people
you thought were true, react uncaringly to you.
The truth is they never were. They were just passing through.
Know in your own heart, the value of you.

I still am afraid, absence of you doesn't mean you're gone.
I create a land space within my head to feel safe,
A beautiful shoreline where the tide never declines,
It just gently laps at the shore. The beach gives way to a gentle slope
of dunes, and a campfire burns between them. Always with a steady
flame,
Warming amber embers, as night overturns day.

I feel you approaching, I hope it's not true.
What would you look like, now I have separated from you.
Would you be the worst monster, I never could imagine.
I peer though the darkness, not really wanting to see,
With relief I see, you are only the size of me.
You approach the fire opposite and I catch you vehemently looking at
me.
I am shocked by what I see. I am looking at a carbon copy of me.
But it's not the same, the eyes are full of scorn, and a sneering,
seething expression lingered where my smiles are often worn.

We circle, the fire our only dividing line.
I have fought you before, but you are stronger.
I must do something different this time.
So, I grab you quickly and pull you
through the flame. I hold you tight. This time it's you that starts to
fight.
I hold you and whisper in your ear,There must be a reason why you
are here,
What have you come to tell me, I'm listening.

You say many things, I fashion they are not true. And even those
who truly care, have off days too. I tell you, there's always hope.
Even though the road is often full of obstacles, we need to push
through.
We continue into the night, sitting on stationary driftwood.
Sometimes we argue, but I remain true. My words are important too.

I awoke at dawn, not even aware I had slept.

The fire was lit, but you were gone. I start to think differently about you,
You were just here to tell me something needed attention in my mind.
No more than an indication, just like physical pain, when I broke my arm.

It could be, purely accepting a given situation, and moving on.
The best way you can. Leaving a person who won't help you stand.
Remain by your values, it will help you through and bring
the right people to you.
Have the confidence to try, things that bring meaning
to your life. If they don't turn out as you planned,
it's still better than not trying at all. That is the worst fall.

If you return, please be a black dog,
I wouldn't tie your leash and leave you somewhere,
As you would only escape and come and find me anywhere.
We could go for a walk. I know a beautiful shore, but this
time it's not on the inside anymore.

If anything the journey with you, has made me a better person,
I just needed to realise it had, a red cross, a destination,
It was never forever, even though I thought at times
to end you, meant me going too.

I reflect in shock, I'm glad I held on,
I wasn't aware that I would go on
to achieve some of the best things I have ever done.
And meet further inspirational people. To reinforce the path I chose
to be on.

I feel like I have absorbed some
Of your strength, parts of you really
were, just myself. My own grief at
lack of control. Frustrating failure,
as my life took a turn that wasn't on any map I held.
Accepting my path was different now, allowed me to
walk forward without looking back.
I know I will have bad days sometimes. It's human.
I will listen to what you say, but instead, think
why are you telling me this way. If you ever become strong again,
and a brief visit isn't your intention. I won't hide you again.
I hope you like my colours, I have many too,
but unlike yours they remain true, and I will

get further help, if I need too.
I sit here now, alone, but content.
My life is becoming a true reflection
Of everything I needed to do.
And the hours I spent ruminating,
are now filled with things that give life meaning.
 My friends are caring. And they know about you.
My chameleon friend, with changing colours,
and never true, but some of those colours were beautiful too,
and never brighter as I slipped from you.

ABOUT THE POEM
"I wrote this after an intense struggle with mental health. It is my story. I wrote a few lines with colours in them, then thought, why don't I carry on. The way you think, especially when extremely low, colours everything you see. It made choosing the title easy."

ABOUT KAREN
Karen was born with noticeable, but mild cerebral palsy, and became a target for verbal bullying when younger. Depression hit fully after her condition caused her health to decline to a degree that she couldn't work anymore. She became medically retired at 36, and lost her career, friends and her mum within a two year period. She felt she had no place in the world, and became devastatingly isolated and lonely. She was self-harming and drinking, but knew she would wouldn't live long if she didn't get help. Therapy (her third over the years), and a free NHS self management programme (EPP) both helped her find understanding friends. She is now a volunteer tutor for that service, and writes frequently.

Poetry by Andrew Nacht

HER OCD
(there and back and there)

Months before the life threatening bony face and total cessation of
behavioural norms
her mind called out for the hard black wind warriors
and so the Algonquin women, always good with their hands,
fashioned snowshoes borrowing the raw material from Munch's, The
Scream -
a shoe for all seasons, she reasoned.

Once the hard black wind warriors were finally recognized for what
they were
an army of ingested fighters struck at the heart of the enemy, forcing
them to retreat.
Alas, palpable relief was threatened by enemy sightings,
the hard black wind warriors having obviously regrouped nearby.
The enemy stalked and taunted its prey before pouncing,
bringing such overwhelming force
that those who loved her were left scratching their head,
amazed that the enemy was seemingly unperturbed
by the expensive hire of Freud's best trained defence force

MENTAL WARD EXIT

She saw herself moaning in pain lying on her back on the hood of the
car
her arm dangling in front of a headlight wondering how hurt she was
and how she got there
until she shook her head to stop the daydream
welcoming the silence from her husband who was driving the car

Now in In the driveway the sound of the car door closing startled her
as she stared at the house, which felt like an enemy, for the first
time.
She imagined thorns strewn across the floor to prick her feet and
confusing funhouse mirrors
waiting to greet her and shook her head again to ward off the dark
thoughts

The welcome home sign was pleasing

triggering a smile in her husband's direction
and the kids were all hugs and kisses
but she was numb,
only capable of going through the motions
without revealing herself

She let out an unseen sigh of relief upon hearing the words 'Mommy is tired'
grateful to her husband for the cover to sink into bed without fanfare.
Her husband closed the bedroom door so the kids
didn't have to hear her muffled crying into the pillow

ANXIETY BIRD

She sees it perched boisterously on her shoulder
with no memory of it not being there,
nary a thought about where it came from
unless she is looking in the mirror.
For a while when she was younger
she was worried about other people potentially seeing it
until she realized it was invisible to the world.
For her, it acts like an organic living thing,
often times directing her actions,
often times informing her reactions to others.
It obviously doesn't require another pillow at night
but the overnight hours are where she minds its presence the most
since it always has a lot to say
provoking distracting thoughts and feelings

FREE

She walked past the automatic doors with purpose
past the nurses, doctors, orderlies and security
and that rancid institutional smell she knew would last
striding toward a hope with no design
an incomplete but glorious mantra running through her head-
'from darkness to light from darkness to light'
for a moment at least the rancid smell
turned to perfume inside a smile she didn't realize she could still produce

ABOUT THE POEM
"The poems are about either my wife or my two sons who have all

struggled with life changing OCD. The poems reference the full gamut of treatment options; from weekly therapy and hospital mental wards, to out of state residential care. As my family's multi challenges continue, I have found great personal solace in writing about the struggles I am presented with on a daily basis. It is imperative that mental health issues find their way into our cultural consciousness and then to those who are in control of the levers of power to potentially ease the stigma and financial burden of mental health care."

Poetry by Jackie Chou

IF THE WALLS COULD TALK THEY WOULD SAY

I watch you lose the flushed cheeks of girlhood
becoming a gray silhouette pacing in the room
lit by the sunlight spilling through the slats
the only thing shimmering in your current life

Becoming a gray silhouette pacing in the room
you have stopped looking forward to waking up
the only thing shimmering in your current life
the blinking cursor on a computer screen

You have stopped looking forward to waking up
wishing to crawl back to dreams of old glories
the blinking cursor on a computer screen
beyond the grasp of your weathered hands

Wishing to crawl back to dreams of old glories
lit by the sunlight spilling through the slats
beyond the grasp of your weathered hands
I watch you lose the flushed cheeks of girlhood

SONG OF A CARE HOME

There is so much unrequited love in the patio
We gather around its moonlit table at night
Congregating from our corners of existence
Our mouths spewing acres of discontent

We gather around its moonlit table at night
Lonely souls with our unstrung music
Our mouths spewing acres of discontent
Our hearts cracked to the point of breaking

Lonely souls with our unstrung music
We try to pick up the pieces like fallen pearls
Our hearts cracked to the point of breaking
Our lives disarranged like fragments of glass

We try to pick up the pieces like fallen pearls
Congregating from our corners of existence

Our lives disarranged like fragments of glass
There is so much unrequited love in the patio

ABOUT THE POEMS
"I am dealing with some difficult issues at the board and care home where I live, which inspired these poems."

ABOUT JACKIE
Jackie is a poet with schizoaffective disorder. Her collection of poetry, *Finding My Heart in Love and Loss*, has just been released.

Poetry by Angela Theresa Masciale

TYRANNY OF THE MIRROR

Avoid glances in window pains
Step not on, turn away from scale
Reflections tyrannical
Mirror, Mirror on the wall whose the fairest
Caught you evaluating the margins of your curves
Abdomen should be flat like pancake
Critical mind calculating
belly too much like bump on road
Slam on the breaks fast, fast, fast
Getting a high from the deprivation
Then revolt revolutionary gorge
Starvation mode ending with binge then purge
Run marathon swim upstream, against river, cycle
Triathlon peddling burned into exhaustion
Hit the button, repeat
Heart living in stomach aching
Pass not the stretch marks
Hand me pasta, pizza, cannoli's, ice cream, cookies
Stay away cookie monster
Laughing at this beached whale
Then the tears
Crack, mirror toss alongside death scale
Waiting scorpion
Turn off the video on zoom
Get off the not so merry go round.

ABOUT THE POEM
"The idea for 'Tyranny Of the Mirror' came from my husband's slate relief sculpture of a woman looking ghastly at herself in a mirror, having distorted the image in her mind. Body dysmorphia is such a common problem for women, as well as men. My own family is rampant with the struggle of obesity and addiction to food and overeating. Personally, I have struggled myself with food body image in my teens and early twenties, and in my work as a Psychiatric-Mental Health Nurse, I have witnessed first hand the devastating effects physically, psychologically and socially of food and body image obsession."

OCD

Color coordinated overly stuffed closet
Hoard, time to let go
Of picking up every piece of lint
On the rug
Go relax in chair
Ignore crooked painting hanging on wall
Let it be so what if it is not
Straight lined
Dishes pots and pans stacked perfectly
Tops left amiss oh no
Even spices perfectly aligned and named
Food perfectly kept separate
Clean counters disinfect how many times a day
Books CD's facing forward names revealed
Alphabetically too
Under the Christmas tree presents
Paper size coordinated
And do not leave your pocketbook on the floor
Put it inside closet so not
To disrupt the designer room flow
Or else the world may spin off it's axis
OCD madness

ABOUT THE POEM
"My OCD poem was inspired by my work in mental health and OCD related to coping with the pandemic. Personally I think I have a hard time letting go of clothes for example - a tendency with OCD - and I am still cleaning the counters at least once a day (not too bad)."

ABOUT ANGELA
Angela maintain a private mental health practice working with adults. She is also a performing singer-songwriter and poet, and has written both poems and songs on the theme of mental health. She has three CD's T*ime Will Tell, Ancient Voices*, and *Take Back the Land*.
W: www.AngelaMasciale.com
FB: @Angela Theresa Masciale

Poetry by Sabiha Afrose

A LOTUS

In the vast universe
A Lotus.

In the vast pond
No Lotus.

In the vast canvas
A colourful flower.

In the vast tub
No flower.

What's going on
Who can give that answer?

The vast universe or pond or tub
Everything is your part of life

The Lotus or colourful flower
It's your beautiful mind.

You can't imagine
How can you make this hut?

It's true
When you feel .

The mind flies
Life enthusiastically rides.

ABOUT SABIHA
Sabiha is based in Bangladesh, and is the author of nine poetry books.
FB: @safrosemuseofwords
YouTube: @safrose_poetic_arts

Poetry by Ronald Finn

JUST ASKING

When you look into my eyes what do you see?
Is it a blank expression where my face should be?
Do you want my life, do you want my soul?
In answer to your question I can honestly say I don't know.

If you saw me begging in the street would you say 'hi'?
Or would you just turn your head and pass me by?
If I asked to be held close would you say no?
Or if I was acting strange, would you just let go?

If I walked into a room, would you smile?
Even attempt to make conversation if only for a little while?
If I died laughing, would you leave my carcass to rot?
Or hang it on a wall as a piece of art to cover a damp spot?

Because in reality it doesn't matter much to me
I'm out of my depth and out of my tree
You can take what little possessions I own
You can walk away but would you occasionally phone?

Would you call the police to get me on my way
Or indeed prosecute me for wanting to stay?
Would you leave me to fend for myself?
Then come back later to find my mortal remains on a shelf?

Way beyond the clouds and high above the sky
I dream one day of flying higher than any bird of nature dared to fly
To bathe in a sea of innocence to cleanse my mind and body so filthy
Though I protest my innocence, there are those who think I'm guilty

ABOUT THE POEM
"This was written when I was reading peoples thoughts and jumping to the wrong conclusions."

DOWNTRODDEN BUT NOT FORGOTTEN

I found myself standing alone surrounded by darkness
Where even shadows feared to tread
Everything got too much and was getting on top of me

I felt perhaps I was better off dead

I sat on a bench and contemplated
Thinking how did it come to this
All alone and persecuted
I felt sure I wasn't going to be missed

In my mind I felt unworthy
I got to the point where I wasn't so sure
Complete strangers would laugh uncontrollably
To the point where I couldn't take any more

People stood by the side of the road pointing at me
Leaving me with the impression I didn't fit in
I walked alone through the streets of uncertainty
While searching for my self-esteem at the bottom of a bin

Sometimes you have to dream the impossible
Hold your head up as you walk across the floor
Let the waves of injustice wash over you
Stripping back the foundations of life to the core

I was caught between a gulf of indecision
Surrounded by idiots with eyes as cold as steel
I allowed myself to be intimidated by the negatives all around me
I was convinced life was an illusion because nothing felt real

Then I took a closer look at the smiling faces
When I peered behind their false personas it was then that I could
see
How they perceived themselves was not my concern
Friends like them I certainly don't need

A bell rang in my head as though it was a wakeup call
It was then that I decided to spread the word
I set out on a mission to create my own reality
Free to choose colours that others would find absurd

Buried deep in my mind there is a garden
With a few swings, a seesaw and a slide
Somewhere to go and collect my thoughts
The truth is out there somewhere but it's hard to see through the lies

ABOUT THE POEM
"This was written when my moods were up and down like a

rollercoaster."

DEMONS

Be strong and wipe those demons from your mind
They have no right to be there they've crossed the line
Live your life for today, and keep those plans for tomorrow
Think positive as you weren't born to live your life in sorrow

Find the time to look inside yourself
A good spring clean can be good for your health
No one has the right to live inside your head
They are no means your friends so wish them dead

We all ask for help from time to time
It's not as though you're committing a crime
Maybe it would help to change your point of view
It's not so much what you say but what you do

Try not to allow yourself to be dragged down
Life can be difficult enough on the merry go round
Everybody is looking for something in their lives
Follow your heart and don't listen to the lies

The good times are there they just need to be had
It's harder to keep smiling than it is to be sad
Count what blessings you have and make of it what you can
No one is perfect, there is no masterplan

ABOUT THE POEM
"This poem was inspired when I was having a particular bad day and decided to give myself a good talking too."

PARADISE

I'd like to welcome you in
But unfortunately my mind is not my own
I thought I'd invite a few friends over
But the ones I have don't want to know

I pass my time watching TV
Occasionally I may turn it on
I might even be brave and open the curtains

If only to find where my mind has gone

I don't know much except the little I know
While everyday feels the same
I'm not really thinking about tomorrow
I'm just trying to get through today

I know I say I don't need no one
But the truth is I do
I may not talk much
But I'd be happy to talk to you

Everyone sees me smiling
But no one sees my pain
I'd do anything to wake from this nightmare
So I can walk amongst you all again

Mood swings affect my wellbeing
I don't see trust I just see lies
It's times like these that I wish I was on an island
My very own little piece of Paradise

A place where the sun always shines
And the tree's gently sway
Where you don't have to think about tomorrow
Just live your life for today

I'd like to take a moment to breathe
I'm desperate to close my eyes
So that when I eventually fall asleep
I'll be living life in my own little piece of Paradise

ABOUT THE POEM
"I was inspired to write this as my 'go to' place when I was feeling overwhelmed."

ABOUT RONALD
Ronald is 65 years of age and lives in London, UK. His interest in writing poetry began twenty years ago, and he had his first piece of poetry published in 2004. The following year he was invited to The Hastings Poetry Festival (2005) to read some pieces from his portfolio. To-date he has had over fifty poems published on different themes in various publications including mental health. His inspiration is drawn from his own personal experiences as well as his observations of others. Ronald doesn't see his illness/disability as a

cross to bear, but more as part of his journey through life and aiding his creative process. His wife is a great support and source of encouragement in whatever he does.
W: www.ronaldfinn.com

Poetry by Thato Mangwegape

MY PAIN

In all ways I could,
I screamed.
In all ways I could,
I prayed.
In all ways I could,
I apologised even when I did nothing wrong.
In all ways I could,
I begged for mercy.

But my mouth was shut.
My tears meant nothing,
All they could see were meaningless tears.

From seeing a reflection of a good looking young man on my mirror,
From seeing a reflection of a confident young man on my mirror,
To seeing a messed and drained soul tied to a dead walking body.

In every possible way I could,
I tried to erase it all
To move on.
But I guess that is why it is called a memory.

My eyes scream out my pain than my mouth
My heart cries out my pain than my eyes could ever
My silence is more loud than my voice could ever be.
Then my smile covers it all.

Everything feels heavy
Everything seems dark
Or maybe my eyes are too teary to see the light.
No one can ever get it.
Every time I try to speak out I stutter.
I, I, I, I, I ... then close my eyes because that's all I can do.
Every time I try to express how feel my sentence never reach an
ending.
It always goes like this,
I feel like I, I, I, I, orrrrrrrr maybe I, I, I, and that's it.
Eyes then get filled with tears.

Will the world get to know of what happened or how I feel?

I feel like I am dead walking,
Or imagining how being dead feels like,
Because I mean, I am not dead.
Or maybe I am.

ABOUT THE POEM
"I was raped before I could be diagnosed with depression - something which I found hard to let the society know of as, I am a boy-child and that could cause nasty comments. When I wrote this poem I was down, I wanted to express how I felt and what happened, but just not in a direct way so basically this poem gives out the message of how I feel, and what happened."

MY PRAYER

When my voice gets tired of screaming,
When my voice can't be heard,
I pray that the message be delivered through my heart,
When my tears dry out,
I pray that the pain in my eyes be seen,

When the world of the living no more makes sense to me,
I pray that you give me strength ,
When you no more hear my voice
Know that I am not tired of calling your name
Rather, I have no energy left in me.

When those I trusted create a distance,
Assure me that I'll have you in my corner
at all times,
Assure me that I am no cry baby,
Help me find comfort in knowing that you will always have my back

When my hands feels tired of clapping for others,
Give me strength so that I continue doing so knowing that my time will come,
When my legs lead me to paths not aligned to your will,
Freeze them
For I, will know that it's a no go direction for me.

Heal my broken heart,
Clear my red eyes,
Redeem my self esteem,
Not forgetting my confidence,

Lord, be with me.
I am running out of my fighting spirit.

ABOUT THE POEM
"Been a rape victim is never easy - at times I find myself even struggling to get up on my bed or even lift a finger. This poem is to express how tired I feel, or felt, how I couldn't cope after I was raped. Therefore it's a poetic prayer letting my God know of all my emotional struggles."

ABOUT THATO
Thato is a 23 years-old from Taung, South Africa, and is still studying. His passion has always been writing, and anything that's poetic. He is a founder of a non-profit unregistered charity project, and finds joy in helping others.
FB: @Thatomangwegape82

Tricia Lloyd Waller's story

I was born into a big family of very loud, very friendly east-enders, and sadly I was nothing like them. I had overgrown tonsils and struggled swallowing so did not eat much, and for my family this was a huge problem as I was always left at the table facing a cold dinner when everyone else had left. My grandad would put pocket money by the side of the plate, which I could take when the plate was clean - but it never was! I realise now that they used food as a way of showing love, but also as a means of control This had far reaching consequences and led to eating problems for the rest of my life.

I used to escape from them through books, especially fairy tales which were often rhyming, and I loved Robert Louis Stevenson's *A Child's Garden of Verses*. I think the patterns of the words, the sounds and repetitiveness was comforting and reliable when everything else was in a state of flux. I also loved singing at school as a class activity, which made me feel as if I belonged somewhere.

My family were incredibly superstitious, so a lot of what we did - especially before we went out and left the house - were repetitive tasks, and often we would lock the front door push it six times, walk to the end of the road, return, and do it again! I always had to go back on the stairs if someone else was coming up or down, and always counted 12 twice, and never number 13, plus many other daft illogical things. My Mum said it was all to do with the war, but my nan said they had always been like it! Certainly now I think my mum had OCD, and she passed this on in the form of routines that I abided by for years.

She was always telling us to behave ourselves or the men in the white coats would come in the van and take her away, and when I was little I used to spend hours looking out of the big windows terrified they were coming.

The family's attitude to mental health was never admit anything because you will be labelled and be unemployable and unmarriageable! So we never talked about ' problems' to anyone.

I still have eating problems, and could happily eat a huge packet of chocolate digestive ... and want more! I have to make myself eat sensibly, but it's hard. I still have body dysmorphia and see myself as fat - although I know I am not. If I am stressed I eat until I feel sick and then I feel guilty as well.

We were taught to get on with things so nobody has helped me, and I have never spoken to anyone in the Health Service - or anyone really - about any problems.

However, I would certainly advise others to talk about their worries, and not bottle them up.

After my first child died I had a whole load more problems to cope with, and when my two daughters were born and I was struggling to cope, poetry really helped. I wrote poems about the way I felt , how much I loved them, and how sorry I was when I had lost my temper with them. I wrote when they were in bed often early in the morning when words were chasing around in my head. I also wrote a load of 'if only' poems for my baby son who died. Interestingly though, none of my children (I now have a son as well) have ever wanted to see anything I have written about them.

I always kept diaries too, and since they don't want those either, have donated them to Great Diary Project based at Bishopsgate Institute for future social history.

I do write a lot of angry poetry as I guess I am still incredibly angry about how I was treated when my son died, and my grief has turned into anger, but I think that it is actually now a big part of me; *your death defines me.'* I think writing poetry is like speaking to someone who really understands. It is also like uncorking a bottle of champagne - it's a way of letting the pressure out and of easing the pain ... at least for a little while.

Poetry by Tricia Lloyd Waller

BREAKING SYMMETRY

Four letters repeating
Again and again and again.
But transformations
Could and can occur

When you introduce
a chaotic code. Unexpected discoveries
around every hidden corner
waiting to enchant and surprise you.

Delicate drawings belie
surreal fictional narrative.
I cannot understand.
Is this junk?

Triplet codes strung together
in viscous flow.
He is afraid of his position.
Too close – engulfed by viscous flow.

Kicking out intruders before
They piggyback upon your silver soul.
Neural pathways materialising
inside your mind.

Schizophrenia, autism, epilepsy.
Iris petals strewn at your feet.
Breaking symmetry.
Four letters repeating.

Is this Hell? Or is this Heaven?
Are you asking me? Mapping inheritance
searching for breadcrumbs in a trail.
Why do you bother?

Do I live? Or am I dead
Intimate acts of cellular recognition.
Physical gesture floods my brain
But where now lays my tomorrow

ABOUT THE POEM
"This poem was written after being inspired by an exhibition at Francis Crick Institute in 2018. This relates to my teenage years which I spent mainly in my bedroom alone listening to sad records with sad lyrics singing and wondering why I had ever been born and what was the point of my life."

ABOUT TRICIA
Tricia has loved words and the magical patterns you can make by rearranging them in different patterns. She has recently had work accepted by *The World of Myth, Wishbone Words* and *Candlelit Magazine.*
Twitter (X): @TriciaJean44
Instagram: @lilyofaday

Poetry by Caila Espiritu

DESERT BODY EXPLORATION

Down
the
Rabbit
Hole
we
go!
Time is yours. Feel free to stroll.
I am the burnt down ghost town, Calico.
Illegible writings echo on fractured walls.
No signs of life besides the wailing waterfalls.
Dry gust hugs your lungs, sand slits your eyes.
Don't you think it's a delightful, deserted sight?
The ground digs into your skin. You whimper.
It consumes you. And together, you wither
Like tumbleweed with no destination,
Our journey ends with no conclusion.
You'll relive the same nine lives
Over and over, day and night.
Welcome
to
the
other
side!

ABOUT THE POEM
"Taking inspiration from the animated film Alice in Wonderland and the song "Calico" by Korean-Australian singer DPR IAN, "Desert Body Exploration" takes the reader on a journey inside the writer's psyche. The poem presents an endless sense of emptiness and disorientation through adventure, physical sensations, and picturesque descriptions of the imaginary abandoned landscape."

Poetry by Gary Marshall

ODE TO ERP

Is it dark where you are?
Has the light faded
And the night won.
Are your thoughts getting darker?
And the night getting blacker?
Compulse no more.
Let the darkness cover you,
Let the night enfold you.
If it's burning it's working.
Walk towards the darkest corner.
Sit in it.
And wait
For the sun to rise.

ABOUT THE POEM
"I'm a 53 year-old who developed OCD at the age of 19 after leaving home for the first time. I have intrusive thoughts, too embarrassing and shameful for me to talk about. I have recently sought professional help through the NHS, as my compulsions no longer worked. This poem reflects my journey of one-to-one therapy, using ERP (exposure, response, prevention). It's a process of exposure to triggers, without doing your compulsions. Terrifying, it was a journey from desperation to enlightenment and realisation. Supported by my wife and family, it's the hardest thing I've ever done, but my therapist was amazing, and has rewired my brain, changing my life."

Poetry by Gary Shulman

YOU CAN'T TELL ME!

You can't tell me you support me
When your choices devastate
You can't tell me that you love me
When your choices seal my fate
You can't tell me you're all about kindness
When your mind has tunnel vision
You can't tell me you're in my corner
When you vote for pure derision
You can't tell me all is how it should be
When you close your heart to diversity
And make it clear for all to see
So don't you DARE claim you love folks like me!

ABOUT THE POEM
"Homophobia is an epidemic and I am personally affected, so I wrote this poem about my emotions on the topic."

IT HURTS

When child becomes parent
Even just for a while
Tears may fill the eyes
Camouflaging the smile
Seeing a parent transformed
Into an infantile state
Presses hard on the nerves
Evokes a possible future fate
This was the strength
In your life long ago
This was the steadfast given
Didn't we all think so?
But time sometimes acts
As a great wrecking ball
Taking a strong human spirit
And making it fall
So life comes full circle
And the child provides care
As they loved you back then
Love you give back albeit with fear

No words need be spoken
How deeply they do appreciate
The time and support given
Aware of the turmoil piling up on their plate
For the pain of parent becoming the child
Is never an end of life goal
Their mind, heart and soul hurting
Wishing their lives remained healthy and whole
But just as they unconditionally loved
When helpless in this world were we
Back that love must be given
Just as unconditionally

ABOUT THE POEM
"Eventually parents age and the child becomes the parent. My spouse and his sister are going through that very difficult transition now and this poem is about that journey."

ABOUT GARY
Gary is a retired professional in the field of support services for vulnerable families caring for children with disabilities.
W: www.garyshulman.jimdo.com

Poetry by Binod Dawadi

MOOD DISORDERS

When someone scold me I,
Can't become excited,
I become fearful and afraid,
When some teachers punish me,
In my school I can't do anything,
My mood always changed,
As well as I can't be normal person,
I can't control my desires and,
My goals,
I can't control my thinking and my dreams,

I am in a tension all the time,
Like as how to earn?
How to become rich?
As well as I am always worried,
About my future,
I am working hard,
But also I can't do anything,
I am so much hopeless sometimes,
In my life sometimes I want to,
Leave this world and die,

Sometimes I need a lover,
So my mood never becomes,
Perfect tensions and happiness,
Rotates in my life,
As well as they change my thinking,
As well as moods for forever,
In this way I am suffering from mood disorders,
I don't know why I can't think,
Like as a normal person but these are,
The problems of the all people.

ABOUT THE POEM
*"The poem is about myself. I can't control my feelings and thoughts.
I am also a artist and a writer. Artist are not like as a common
people. They always think of impossible things. This life is challenging
me to be successful. I am trying, but I get many tensions and
problems which I am sharing through this poem. It relates to my
dreams and my life."*

ABOUT BINOD

Binod is Nepalese. He has a master's degree in Major English and is the author of *The Power of Words.* He has worked on more than 1000 anthologies, and has been published in various renowned magazines.

Madhavi Tiwary's story

Allow me to share my story of how even people close to a suffering individual, can subject themselves to irreparable mental trauma due to either ignorance or failure to comprehend the disorder of the loved one.

My experience with my mother's dementia started about ten years back.

This specific phase emerged when my mother would smile innocently and ask if I had met my aunt - followed by a single, or at times double repetition of the same question. Sometimes I would answer calmly, but at times irritation in my voice could not be missed.

An year or two passed with similar episodes repeating themselves with similar reactions from me.

Then, such episodes multiplied into many, and more frequently too. My irritation reached new levels. I could not understand why mother would like to know that day's date about five times a day. The only reason I could think of was that she took sadistic pleasure in irritating me. Mother would only look with blank eyes, completely unable to think of a reason for my annoyance. She would ask the date one more time. I would stare at her angrily one more time.

A couple of years later my visits to my mother became a sore battle between us. Mother would ask when my return flight was ,followed by a dozen repetitions of the same question on any single day. Despite all my academic accolades, my claims to inspiring audiences, my so called leadership prowess, I would lose my temper even at the first repetition of anything uttered by her. By the dozenth repetition, I would be so agitated that I would threaten to cut short my visit immediately. Mother would just crouch on the sofa with eyes blurred with some water.

Approximately, in the middle if those last ten years, my brother consulted a doctor about mother's general health and was told that she was suffering from dementia. The information was duly conveyed to all her daughters, including me. I considered myself well informed – till I actually spent some time with mother. Mother would talk about this and that – normally - just as she did all her life. Nothing seemed to have changed much, except that on some occasions she would repeat herself multiple times, that too without warning. I would be taken off guard and would react exactly the same way as I had been doing all these past five years – with displeasure followed by stern anger. This would invariably result in the same blank and bleak look on her face.

Mother's misery increased without anyone really noticing it. Five more years of such battle led her to become almost completely quiet, as if she had lost any will to talk. Her days passed sitting on the chair, staring at the walls without a spoken word.

Then, one morning, during the recent pandamic lockdowns, she became silent forever. My brother was alone to say the final goodbye. My visit was not to be – this last time.

A time of introspection followed. I suffered terrible pangs of remorse. The realization flashed like a whip that mother never intended to repeat things. She was not even aware that she was doing anything of the kind. To her knowledge, she was saying those things for the first time. Imagine to have met with such ire! How heart-stabbing that must have been. She underwent this agonizing experience for more than ten years. She lost her voice. She lost her will.

Despite having been told that my mother suffered from dementia, I somehow could never digest or actively remember it. Her conversations were so normal otherwise that every repetition sounded like intentional repetition. How callous, how criminally foolish of me to have behaved like that! The realization how much I hurt my mother is going to deep prick me for the rest of my life. My ignorance of my mother's dementia in the first five years, and later my carelessness towards the disorder, not only hurt my mother, it is traumatic for me every time I think of my unforgivable behaviour.

So, all you sons and daughters out there, I plead you, consciously try not to hurtfully silence your parents, who are the unfortunate victims of dementia.

Poetry by Linda M. Crate

NO ONE WANTS THE TRUTH

everyone talks about mental health,
but still people find ways to
undermine it;

you wouldn't let your foot rot off your
body without doing preventative care

so why should you mind be any different?

there's only so much one can hold in
before they feel like they'll explode or fall
apart at the seams,

why should we be expected to unravel
in quiet spaces where we don't disturb anyone?

everyone needs community,
no one should be forced to endure life
on their own;
strength and circumstance can fail
us all—

yet people just expect people who struggle
with their mental health to press on,
never mentioning their struggle;

that's why i sometimes tell people i am fine
when they ask how i am even if i'm not

because no one wants the truth—when you're struggling.

ABOUT LINDA
Linda's works have been published in numerous magazines and anthologies both online and in print. She is the author of 11 poetry chapbooks and four micro-poetry collections.

Poetry by Antoni Ooto

MY LAST STAND
(for Jackie Trobia)

They say I suffer no fools...that's true.

Trapped in different waiting rooms carrying the same pain...always pain. From doctor to doctor in a lifetime of failing promises...I've listened. With countless medications and years of tests... I've tried.

On the day I was told my mind would also be failing, I took back power. With a clear head, and my last traces of strength, I designed a strategy that never allowed weakness the advantage. Slowly I separated from medical hope.

Once, a mentor, a teacher, now I need to show others how this final battle will go. It is the right time.
Consoling family and friends is the hardest part. Still, it's a finish to a life already ending.

Some accept, and others won't. But those who understand...forgive.

ABOUT THE POEM
"'My Last Stand' is a tribute to our good friend who soldiered through so much that was painful in her life. She was indeed a warrior, who with a sense of humor and without complaints, made the world safer when she was around."

ABOUT ANTONI
Based in New York, USA, Antoni's work is widely published globally in print, online, and in anthologies. His poems reflect special memories, a love of nature, and the listening to life's smaller moments. He is also a well-known abstract expressionist artist whose paintings are collected throughout the US.
Linkedin: @antoniooto

Poetry by Gabriela Docan

INVISIBLE BATTLES
Inspired by one person's experience with mental illness

Neighbours must get a terrible fright
When they hear me shouting at night
From the top of my lungs, very loud.
I don't yell at myself, but at a crowd.

I'm also scared, but I cannot tell
Spirits come to seek help or rebel.
I shout at them to leave me alone
Or I say prayers until they're gone.

I can't turn on radio or TV,
Because spirits jump out to argue with me,
To punish me for something I've done wrong,
The physical torture can last all day long.

My cat gets frightened and hides away
Shivering under the bed, where she stays
For long hours, sadly without food,
Keeping herself in solitude.

I plan to shower and take my meds,
Put on pyjamas, brush teeth - but instead
I lose track of time, get confused,
Fall asleep, tired with mind bruised

With clothes on, without showering, eating,
In agony after the spirit's been pinching me.
In the morning, I search for my cat;
She must be somewhere hidden in this flat.

I'm in agony but out of painkillers,
Have to get Codeine and ready dinners,
If only I could step outside of my flat
And not freeze in fear on the doorstep mat.

The severe anxiety launches attacks
I wish I could fight off or take a step back.
Paralyzed by a panic I struggle to bear,
I feel a lump in my throat, gasp for air.

It's hard to describe the claws under which
Minds get injured; there is no visible stitch.
The truth is I struggle with everyday life
But against all odds, somehow, I survive.

ABOUT THE POEM
*"Invisible battles is inspired by a former service user's experience
with schizophrenia and severe anxiety, who I used to support when I
worked in mental health as an Outreach Day Service Officer. The
poem is based on the person's own narrative and depicts fragments
from her daily harrowing battles, which she shared with me. The
intention behind writing this poem is to throw a glimpse into how
schizophrenia and severe anxiety can manifest and impact on
someone's life. Hallucinations are a common symptom of
schizophrenia. They can occur at any of the five senses and can be
either visual, auditory, olfactory, gustatory, or tactile. The person the
poem refers to has strong visual, auditory and tactile hallucinations
that are perceived as 'spirits' who come to visit, ask for help or
physically punish the person for wrong doings. They often cause
distress, anxiety, physical pain and interference with everyday
activities and night sleep."*

BLISSFUL MOMENT

I close my eyes, breathe in and out with calm,
Silence the world, in search for a soul balm.
Time and space dissolve. I relax, unwind,
Tame all worries, instating peace of mind.

I clean the grime spoiling days with dirt,
Exorcize demons that make me get inert,
Conquer struggles that make me distraught,
Lingering often in body, soul and thought.

I breathe in slowly, stop and search within,
Wrap myself with calm, stop the mental spin.
To surrounding beauty, I open my soul wide,
For rivers of tranquillity to flow inside.

I drown worries before starting to crowd,
Unearth my spirit: powerful, unbowed!
There is nothing now that I need or miss:
This moment is so peaceful, simply a bliss!

First published in POETICA #2 (2020).

ABOUT THE POEM

"Blissful moment is a motivational poem that stems from my work experience in mental health and acts as an example of positive self-talk. Positive self-talk are those things that we tell ourselves that uplift, motivate and keep us going. The poem highlights the importance of breathing in relaxation and how we become more receptive to the surrounding reality once we are calm and in a good frame of mind. It describes the attempts to balance daily worries and struggles – that constantly chip at our fragile mental health - with the so much yearned tranquillity and inner peace. Maintaining good mental health in life is an ideal, a challenge, as tricky as walking on a tightrope. The poem conveys the belief that people are at their essence powerful and unbowed, not easily defeated, able to overcome struggles and experience moments of true bliss."

ABOUT GABRIELA

Gabriela is a humanist, poet, beauty hunter, nature lover, chronic daydreamer, over thinker and traveller. She currently lives in Watford, UK. Her poems have appeared in *Poetry for Mental Health, Agape Review, MindFull, Stripes, Writer's Egg Magazine, Spillwords.com* and various themed print anthologies published by MacKenzie Publishing, The Ravens Quoth Press, Sweetycat Press, Clarendon House Publications and *The Poet*.

Poetry by Gargi Saha

MENTAL ABUSE

My mind is like a white paper
That blots the black and the white
Semantics and non meanings
Syllables,morphemes,words, phrases

Which to be considered intended?
Which unintentional, just a slip of tongue?
Meanings envelop meanings
A layer within another engulfed

No circumference, no contours
Which ones to ignore, which to imprint?
Which ones to recall,which to forget?
Speechless trauma sailing in an abyss of
Infinity

Silence spreads its shadowing sheath
And awaits the hour of justice
Is it justified?
To scratch someone by the invisible, deepest,darkest scars in the
psyche?

ABOUT GARGI
Gargi lives in India. She is a creative writer, and has published two
poem books, *The Muse in My Salad Days*, and *Letters to Him*. She
recently received the Rabindranath Tagore Memorial Award, and the
Independence Day Award for poetry. She is a member of various
poetry groups on Facebook, and presently she edits several scientific
research papers.

Interview with John F. Zurn

John's experiences with mental illness began when he was 14 years-old. Depression, manic episodes, psychotic breaks and alcohol abuse resulted in hospitalisation, homelessness and jail. Now on the road to recovery, a combination of counselling, medication and creativity has completely transformed his life.

Thank you for talking to me John. When did your first experiences with mental health begin?

My experiences with mental illness really began when I was 14 years-old, growing up in upstate New York. At that time, the legal drinking age for alcohol was 18; so 16 year-old teenagers could make fake identification and buy alcohol, and 14 year-old students could buy from them. So I drank every weekend, and all summer throughout high-school. But, alcohol notwithstanding, I was also a pretty good student, played the trumpet, and ran cross-country and track. Eventually, I was awarded a partial scholarship to St. John Fisher College in Rochester, New York. But, in the summer of my freshman year, I had a life-changing experience: while I was jogging around my uncle's resort, I became violently ill with severe cramps. By the time I arrived at the hospital the next day, I had to have an emergency appendectomy and, back in 1974, if my appendix would have burst, I surely would have died. For the first time I realized that death was both real, and inescapable, and over time became obsessed with death. Depression began to overwhelm me and I lost interest in almost everything.

And then what happened?

Eventually, when the depression finally lifted, I experienced what could be described as three consecutive 'manic' episodes. During these 'psychotic breaks', I deliberately raced my thoughts as fast as possible, seeking answers to my questions about death. During these episodes I was hospitalized for months at a time, and since my symptoms were manic, I was also consistently misdiagnosed as a consumer (patient) with schizophrenia. Then, two years later, I finally made a very serious suicide attempt and was a patient in intensive care for about a week. Ironically, however, that desperate act provided the vital information needed to correctly reach my diagnosis of bipolar disorder.

How did things develop from there?

I eventually got into very serious trouble. I hired a cab from Elgin (Chicago) to Champaign - a journey of around 160 miles, costing two-hundred and fifty dollars - so I could visit my brother. Since my brother was more interested in studying than seeing me and partying, we quickly parted company, and I ran out of money. A university counselor gave me a bus ticket back to Chicago, and when I arrived at about 2 a m, I began wandering the downtown streets directing and blocking traffic because I firmly believed I was the fifth Beatle, and that one of the group members was coming to pick me up. People from a nearby bar threw bottles at me, and a man tackled me to the ground. Before long, the police came and I was taken to the psych division of Cook County Jail, called Cermak.

What was that like?
To be honest, it was a vicious, brutal place. After about four or five days, I was pushed out the front door by two officers. I had nowhere to go, had no belt or shoes, and was told to "behave myself." I wandered around the Chicago area again for a while. I was then re-incarcerated in another section of Cook County Jail. This jail was also a violent world of savagery and despair. To be honest, I didn't think I would survive it.

How did things start to change?
Acceptance, for me, has been a process over time, and I finally realized that taking medication was a safety issue. Taking medication, and going to counselling, was a very humbling experience for me as for many people, including myself, taking medicine and receiving counselling was a sign of weakness and a lack of courage. But they are not, they are a road to recovery, and now, my bipolar disorder no longer rules my relationships nor dominates my life. Instead, it has made me a more creative and compassionate person. By accepting my illness, I have become more disciplined and productive because I better understand and manage my thoughts and feelings. With the help of my wife, Donna, I now cherish a life I once considered worthless.

Generally, how do you think poetry, writing and being creative can help people with mental health challenges?
Creativity helps redirect delusional impulses, so we express ourselves in more socially acceptable ways. For example: writing stories and poems may help channel and manage this energy into something tangible before it overwhelms. A number of us with bipolar disorder have a high degree of intelligence. However, we can't handle a lot of stress, partly because of the anxiety that is often part of the diagnosis. Creativity, like writing and painting, for example, are practiced with no one else around. Working alone, we can fully engage our intelligence without any outside pressure. In fact, the

only stress we usually experience is the pressure we put on ourselves. In addition, it is very difficult to find any job that has high intelligence and low stress. Creativity gives us a chance to build our self-confidence, maintain a genuine sense of purpose, and overcome boredom.

Creativity expands awareness because, in the process of writing, we can grow spiritually by developing self-discipline. After creating a poem or story, we become a different, more mature person. In other words; thoughts and actions that once led to mental illness like 'wrong turns' and 'crash landings' no longer influence us. We have evolved to a new expanded level of understanding.

And lastly John, how has poetry, writing and creativity helped you personally recover?
For me, creativity also provides a sense of closure, and helps resolve festering emotions and unresolved conflicts. I think about a problem, such as a terrible memory like Cook County jail, and then I write about it, and then I often experience a cathartic feeling of moving past the experience. Sometimes when I'm depressed, I can capture the actual feeling, then describe it, and then let it go.

"Creativity keeps my mind positively occupied, so it doesn't have the chance to focus on doubt, anxiety, and restlessness."

Poetry by John F. Zurn

LURKING

Anxiety is always near
lurking in my consciousness.
It's sometimes more than I can bear
and makes me feel incompetent.
Like a shadow in my life,
it haunts me like a curse.
I never know when it will strike
or when things may get worse.

WHERE I MIGHT BE GOING

Everyday turns on my moods,
and thoughts are so uncertain.
Some mornings I can own the room,
and everything seems perfect.
But there are times when I believe
that love is just a slogan.
I can't explain the way I feel
or where I might be going.

TRAPPED

Awakening at peace each day,
my mind leans into thinking.
The presence then has gone away
replaced by my ambition.
By nightfall I have trapped myself,
and everything feels crooked.
I feel that I am someone else
who has no living spirit.

PILLS AND RULES

If could give up all these pills,
my mind would be wide open.
No longer cornered by the rules,
I'd thrive and not be coping.

But either I would lose my way
in some role I might perform,
or else despair would end the play
with no shelter from the storm.

CHAOS

When chaos reigns inside my head,
I know that I am terrified.
The racing, roaring thoughts that spread
are like a spinning, flooding death.
So when I'm streaking into space
and feel my brain about to burst,
I recognize I need to wait
and let the chaos do its worst.

ABOUT JOHN
John has been faced with the challenges of bipolar disorder and
anxiety disorder for his entire adult life. Over the years he gradually
learned that: medication, physical exercise, meditation and creative
writing were vital for his long term recovery. Despite this challenge,
he still managed to work as a teacher and counselor for over thirty-
five years. Now retired, he has more time to write and publish poems
and stories. John was born in upstate New York and has an M.A. in
English. He has been married to his wife, Donna, for over 40 years.
W: www.portalstoinnerdimensions.com
FB: @writerjohnfzurn

Poetry by Joan McNerney

SHADOWS

This day unrolls before us.
I want to scream out against
flat skies, tear up coarse air.

Put through my paces
with long lists of minutiae.
Acrid weariness crawls up spine.
My eyelids droop shut.

Today pulls us forward...
pushing yesterday aside.
Each night coming faster, faster.
Winds blowing stronger, stronger.

Cats howl in cold circles as
ragged leaves cling to boughs.
Rain falls like ebony ink
under small pools of light.

Darkness gathers close...
my own silhouette black and
tall slants downward following
me through the long night.

ABOUT THE POEM
*"This poem is about the tedium of pushing yourself forward through
another flat day. Flat days are familiar to those with vegetative
depression."*

SICK SICK SICK

the universe is
a labyrinthine in my
ear ear ear.
I am deaf from it
there is no sure
melody in these
crazy strains.

deaf deaf deaf
dumb blinded
loosening mind
for just one moment
to a maze of human
dilemma absurd.

gone gone gone
everything is
senselessly gone
running thru rooms
marked no exit
crying out in
no voice.

dance dance dance
on the barbed wire
of time feet raw
raw raw bleeding
blood blood blood.

ABOUT THE POEM
"This describes the panic of coming from a dysfunctional family filled with both alcoholism and mental illness. Add poverty to the list. I had to support myself during my last year of high school. This was when females were only paid 40 cents compared to the male dollar."

TUMBLING

through time as
I lay thinking always
remembering

how this crap shoot of life
crushed my dreams spinning
me into an unlikely comedy

listening to a busy world
trains, ships, planes,
never ending hiss of cars

revved up motorcycles
loud televisions, shouts,
radios, alarms, sirens

shifting memories
over in my mind trying
to find some pattern

finally night, long, deep
and black covers me with
blankets of forgetfulness

ABOUT THE POEM
*"Looking back at it all, some things are gained but many lost.
Growing older now and wondering do I belong anymore to this busy
world."*

GLOOM

Night paints my room black
while I listen to raindrops.

So many dark secrets
written in its black ink.

Night is my highway to
lost dreams. Dogs in the alley
barking at the wind.

ABOUT THE POEM
*"Lying in bed at night, I hope to escape through dreams. Are you also
lost? How many others lie awake listening as darkness covers them?
"*

ABOUT JOAN
Joan has been the recipient of three scholarships. She has recited her
work at the National Arts Club, New York City, State University of
New York, Oneonta, McNay Art Institute, San Antonio and the
University of Houston, Texas as well as other distinguished venues. A
reading in Treadwell, New York was sponsored by the American
Academy of Poetry. Published worldwide in over thirty five countries,
her work has appeared in literary publications too numerous to
mention. Four Best of the Net nominations have been awarded to
her. Her titles include: *The Muse in Miniature, Love Poems for
Michael, At Work* and *Light and Shadow.*

Poetry by Mary Bone

THE HEART DRUM

A heart drum is a steady beat.
We have heard it through the ages,
resounding in canyon walls-
echoes from a distant drum.

MEMORY LANE

Looking through my hospital window,
I see patients having a picnic.
There are children playing on Memory Lane.
With my heart on my sleeve, as i think back.
I am still the girl with the toothless grin.

SONGBIRD'S TRILL

A melody outside my window-
beautiful music from a Songbird's trill.
It takes my mind off sorrow and pain,
knowing I may be hearing the serenade,
for a short time, outside my windowsill.

ABOUT MARY
Mary's poems have been published at *Mental Health.Org, Spillwords, Visual Verse, Literary Yard, Active Muse Journal, The Academy of the Heart and Mind, Words of the Lamb* and other places.

Poetry by Sam C. Smith

INNER STRENGTH

Maybe she's okay.
She can stay.

For now.
Not forever,
just as long as she needs,
while I'm healing.
She's helped me cope,
manage through life's turmoils.

No one else notices her,
but she's there,
keeping going.
She's there
to help take me through the motions,
until we reach the other side.

The time will come,
where we will part gently.
She will be there again
when I need her,
like how I need her now,
but there will always be a part of her
inside me,
to help me along the way.

On my journey.

We're all affected
by many fragments of life.
You can create beautiful things
out of broken pieces.

We find people along the way
on our journeys.
They can be the most supportive people,
but at the end of the day,
they'll never get it.
They'll never truly get you.
Maybe most of you
if you're lucky,

but not all of you.

Because it's your life,
not theirs.

They can't fully understand
someone else's life
when they haven't lived it.

Inner strength
is your most powerful tool.

It's there,
even if you can't see it.
Even if you can't feel it.

When you just want to give up
and sink into your bed,
never to be seen again.

It's there.

ABOUT THE POEM
"This poem is about healing and beginning to learn self-compassion rather than mental health being your worst enemy. It represents mental health being a fluid journey, shaped by the life-lessons we gain with each experience, and the acceptance that life will never be 'perfect,' or without its challenges, but there's still a lot of good in the world. It's about realising you have to be on your side for recovery, that there's hope - even if it feels like everything is constantly crashing down. Ultimately it conveys the sudden epiphany on the importance of determination and self-perseverance to manage through all the pain and adversity, so you can inspire and empower others going through similar struggles."

STRANGER

Who have you become

Who is she
That face in the mirror
staring back at me

That's you.

Physically.

She scares me, but not enough
to do anything about it.
She's here to protect you
from all that hurt,
it's not going to happen.
Ever again.

She won't let it.

They took her heart
and smashed it into pieces.

But she's not like how I was.
How I used to be.

I want the real me back.
None of this is me
Another mind,
but my body.

This is for the better,
to protect you.

It all feels so wrong.

Shutting people out.
Cutting people off
Keeping life private,
not letting anything out
that could be used against you.
Stay out of everyone's way,
out of harm's way.
Then nothing can happen.
There's nothing left
to fuel the fire.
No ammunition.
Nothing that can jump out of the flames
to burn you.

What to say,
what not to say.
How to act,
what to do,
what not to do.

So many impossible rules.
It had to be done.

They had their chance.

What happened was unforgivable.

I need her for surviving the day,
but I want the old me back.
Where I was authentically me,
honest,
polite,
all of the things.

Not perfect.

She definitely wasn't perfect.

I don't want to get used to this.
I'm becoming someone I'm not.
This isn't me.

I want back.

ABOUT THE POEM
"I wrote this poem during a time of ongoing trauma, and was struggling to come to terms with my own defence mechanisms and thought patterns I had developed. It was a time of longing for the version of myself before I experienced such a deep degree of hurt, pain and disappointment by many people in my life who should have uplifted me."

N.T. Anh's story

IN THOSE QUIET MOMENTS

Back in 2019, many people asked me why I didn't ride my motorbike anymore. The simple answer was: "I'm lazy." The real answer was I had a hard time fighting the urge to crash myself and die a brutal death.

I've always wondered how "I" came to be. How my body, my brain, and this white phantom thing people call soul came into existence. How they respond, react, and affect one another to operate what is "I."

Even now it's difficult for me to admit it. That I have struggled with mental illness throughout my life. When I was younger, myself and everyone around me passed this off as a part of my character. This dramatic, melodramatic side of myself. But I don't believe a person's character would want to drive them to death.

When did it all start? I wasn't sure. All I knew was the feeling. The guilt. A strong sense that I am at fault for everything. That I was unloved, unwanted.

There should have been a reason. But perhaps there needn't. And since I didn't understand why I felt such a way, I punished myself for it. Perhaps I just wanted to justify my moods and behaviours. Because, truly, I didn't have a reason.

But I started losing the things I loved.

At first, it was like an "aha" moment. As if I knew all along that my life was a mess. But then it became too much. Sometimes I begged life not to take from me anymore. But everything was still falling apart.

I began cutting myself. It felt okay. Neither good nor bad. I did it simply to feel something. To chase away this intangible pain that I couldn't pinpoint in my body. Maybe there wasn't any pain at all. Maybe I was just imagining it so that I could feel, special. Different. Worthy of love.

How I feared to be ordinary. But utterly am ordinary myself. Because I am not excluded from any human experience. I failed. Being isolated. Unwanted. Unloved. Hated. Exploited. Abused. Abusing. Reacting. Hating. Wanting ...

Yet having emotions is the most damnable, unreasonable nature of a human being in the age of capitalism. We all have to hide. Be inconspicuous. And so, to be loved and accepted by a loveless society, I put on a smile when I was told to. I can hide but I cannot unfeel the anger when people say I looked happy. Carefree. Young. Privileged. I didn't look like someone who suffers. Because suffering is the opposite of love, happiness, and success. To look in pain is to set myself up for failure, further suffering, and unworthiness of love.

So, I had to laugh. Laugh even harder. Because outside of this laughter, what else did I have? In *Animal Joy* Nadir mentioned a person who laughs when they open up about their disturbing past. Laughter, cry, a fist to the wall, are all reactions. Just reactions. They have no positive or negative connotation. So who decided that laughter entails happiness? And what exactly is happiness? Can we only be happy if we laugh?

At the point when the pain reached its pinnacle, I was completely disconnected. I remembered nothing but the moments of ending, the moments when I lost, lost those who were precious to me. My memories, how detailed were. How they haunted me. Yet I couldn't see myself in my recollection. I didn't have a face. I didn't know what I looked like. Even when I stood in front of the mirror, I was seeing somebody else.

So I scrambled for what was left of me. I looked for pictures of myself as a child. When I was a month old, three years-old, ten, twelve, and twenty. I wondered if it was the distance or the nostalgia that retrieved a sense of compassion in me.

Who would hurt this child? But I did. I cut into my wounds. I weaponised my sufferings to tyrannise myself, to control and prevent the child in me from ever trusting and hoping.

Why? What did I do wrong? I was there through everything, all of them, why was I beaten again for being in pain?

I don't want to be a victim. I don't want to be a tyrant. I wanted to ...sleep. I wanted to not feel. And maybe the only way to not feel is to feel, every detail of it, every moment when I could hear my heart break. Because I had tried so many ways to forget, to move on, except to feel.

I retraced the experience. I write.

And I cry every time I write. Naturally, I must have been sad, to have relived those painful memories. Yet how absurd it was that I found happiness every time I put my heart down to paper. I later came to understand what I was doing then, writing for hours and hours, symbolising, making stories and crafting proses, was processing my trauma.

I wrote my life yet I was standing far away, observing my life through the lens of a reader. And by doing so I could see everything that happened objectively and find purpose, even beauty in the suffering I have been through.

Perhaps, to be more precise, it wasn't happiness that I felt, if we consider it as opposed to sadness by convention. I felt peace. Quietness. I wasn't running when I wrote. The rat-run for love, happiness and success couldn't reach the safe space I created with my writing. I felt healed. And the appreciation I felt for myself, by myself, and with myself, was free and beyond the eyes of the others.

A friend once asked me if I ever find myself dependent on writing as a kind of lifesaver. I believe all writers do, at some point. But if this state continues, their inspiration and eventually, their writing will die out. The tortured writer is but a doomed character, forever mystified and worshipped, but never truly understood. And isn't that similar to the elusive love that I had spent all my life chasing after?

I gave up being happy. I lost. I am not loved, not wanted in the way people expected me to be. I am guilty of having too many feelings. I was punished to put on an empty mask for everyone's sake. I suffered and I suffer still, perhaps I suffer, will. But at least I was true, always true in every word I have written. And the truth requires no effort. It flows with ease and tranquillity.

I don't want writing to carry around this enormous responsibility to make me happy. It needn't make me happy. My writing isn't something I own, it grows along with me. It may reflect every living experience of mine, but it isn't the reason, the excuse why I may continue to suffer. I suffered because I had an idea of how life should be yet it failed me. And this eternal chase between fantasy and reality is innate to all living creatures with emotion.

Writing is a gateway. It brings out a silence in me that allows me to process and proceed with my story. Only in writing, where I stand far away and observe reality from a bird's eye view, do I draw the line between these polarities and find a place for myself. A space. A quiet moment, where I am myself but also see myself, writing.
About the author

ABOUT N.T. ANH
N.T. Anh is a Vietnamese writer, graduated with a Master's in English Literature from the University of Glasgow. Anh is currently pursuing her second Master's in Psychology while working as an English lecturer. And by night, she still continues to write and dive into the fictional world of her own.
Instagram: @anhphily

Poetry by Jamie Gannon

SOME DAYS

Sometimes
I am unwell mentally
And I guess a lot
Because it is really hard to tell–
I know everyone is unwell

sometimes

But they haven't had their
shoelaces taken away
Or lived behind a locked door
On a floor with an armed guard
And the door to your room is
cellophane and
the shower curtain imagined is
dangled from earbuds confiscated

It's hard to tell if you're ok
But you've been locked up
with such gentle recurrence

It is just so difficult
To know
When hurting yourself
Is happening

The gentle pull of self
by bootstraps taken
Defeat awash in loss

You kind of think
You're just a suicide

But only some days

EAST/WEST

He was not a pretty man
But there was once a kindness

In his eyes

In life
You get locked up
For the hate you apply
To yourself

Some do it with drug
Some do it with drink
Some do it with blood

But we all are locked up
In a pretty tight hole
With multiple check-ins
And locked doors—
Real, serious locked doors

Irv and I argued about which way
The large glass-paned
hospital window
was facing:

I said West
Irv said East

I said West
He said East

I said West
Irv said East

And at the end of the day,
He was coming off a long drunk
And I was only once
again suicidal

The window was facing West

But we both wore the same gowns...

The argument lasted an hour or two.

Or three.

Hospital windows don't reveal much--

other than you are in a hospital

Again

But I will remember him for
the rest of my life.
Maybe next time
Irv and I will be
On a different floor
And a different window
Will reveal a different sun

THIMBLES AND THREADS

Sometimes
we survive by
thimbles and threads
Where an act of kindness or
the gentleness of touch
Can separate here from there

I broke my heart to
find my body
and
I broke my body to
find my heart

And
sometimes
You die of wounds
A day
A month
A year
Several
Then
More

Died of wounds
On a dark night
forever ago
But always now

ABOUT THE POEMS
"These poems were written and edited from the 4th floor of the

community hospital. The 4th floor is both locked and secure - it is suicide watch."

ABOUT JAMIE
Jamie is a professor of writing and journalism. She once came upon a beautiful, life-changing anthology, *Against Forgetting*. The anthology's premise was simple: how to use poetry to confront personal, physical, and political trauma. Poems as civil disobedience; poetry as defiance. She is currently finishing her dissertation and dreaming of the Italian countryside.

Poetry by Christopher Martin

CANADIAN WILDFIRES

Like the boy king made Matryoshka doll,
Dragged back through reeds to a glass bardo,
Scoliosis snakes my spine like a whip;
Buckled under the weight of a secret
Grief, traumas knotweed, spreading
Chinese whispers
Of memory
To he who listens; black birds twisting
Under the radar, even in a private mirror;
Pot bound—the heart in-growing—
Things moving in hopeless directions.

ABOUT CHRISTOPHER
Christopher is a poet and Buddhist living by the mouth of the Tyne on the north east coast of England. His work has featured in various publications and events. An author with the Black Cat Poetry Press, his debut collection is due out 2024.
FB: @theblackcatpoetrypress

Poetry by Nicola Vallance-Ross

ROBUST

A never ending up and down, low than high, bright lights, but more often dark. A happy, often followed by insatiable sadness.

A bright, rich pond.
A screaming desert.

I received this illness from you, Dad.
No shame though.

My forgiveness would be an unjust blame. We can't contain genetics, we can't outrun this paradoxical stain.

I'll never be the same -

as the ninety nine out of one hundred.

The trees bleed when I'm agitated, the world swirls, fast and furious.

I'm one step ahead, or a million behind.
A power house of a woman - or a smudge in my dark, beautiful smelling bedroom.

But with this illness comes a unique bubble of euphoria, a flowing torrent of elation and unrivalled self motivation. Creativity and empathy. My open eyes to the suffering of this world, a uniqueness to my soul.

So I don't need to forgive Dad, I will appreciate the moods that blessed us.

For my unique perspective on this world.
For teaching me acceptance.
For passing down a paradoxical curse

that overcoming ensures I'm completely and empathetically

robust.

Poetry by Princess Joe-Igbuzor

POEM 1

I finally understood why I
always criticised Disney animations.
I wasn't cynical about the prince
rushing in to save a distressed
damsel or that they both rode away
on a horse into the sun.
I was hurt, and my insecurities bled
through the snide remarks I made.
Because when I screamed till my voice
became hoarse, no prince
barreled through the doors, no
happy ending in sight, just the bitter truth
of my reality jolting me up like a splash
of ice-cold water.

POEM 2

Cherish your solace,
but beware of the boisterous
city noise.
Learn to find comfort
in your space but do not
be alone for too long a time.
Interact with people but
Guard your words.
Take in everything but
pay great attention to detail.
Life was all about the
balance that you establish.

POEM 3

I can see just fine in the dark
tunnel that is my mind. You might
stumble along the way and maybe
fall here and then. But I wouldn't
No one knows a house better than its
owner, especially one who had inhabited

for years. I didn't require sight for
getting by in here, I knew each dent,
each crack and each story that lay behind
it. I once found these cracks ugly now they
remind me of every beautiful piece of me.

POEM 4

I haven't figured out
who I was yet.
I am conflicted between
multiple choices.
I want to go out,
feel the sun kiss my skin,
dress up pretty, smile brightly,
Kiss that random stranger.
But at the same time, I want
to stay home, my legs prepped
up on the couch, my phone off,
my nose is stuck in a book.
And then I want to be
dancing the night away
at a club, the loud music pumping
through me as the alcohol
burns down my throat, and
leaves a bitter taste
in its wake.
But instead, I lay beneath
the sheets and live
out all these
different personas
through my mind.

ABOUT THE POEMS
*"By writing predominantly about mental health, my focus is to de-
stigmatize the mystic aura behind mental health, and reduce it into
concepts that people can understand in everyday life."*

ABOUT PRINCESS
Princess is a Nigerian Law student who is passionate about mental
health and women's rights.
Blog: https://princesstegajoewriter.art.blog/
Instagram: @Write_rspace
LinkedIn: @Princess Joe-Igbuzor

Poetry by Collen Molahlehi

IMPOSTER SYNDROME

I wear these words like a knight wears his armour,
I hide behind each simile that has lost its smile
And dig myself into each metaphor that lends me its roar
It's hard to see just how much each line rips away
from the inner confines of this tired soul
I scribble words until an empty rose stem remains,
and fallen petals line the trenches
of the lost conversations I wasn't strong enough to have
I am a wolf in sheep's clothing
Drowning in the very words meant to save me
An imposter who hopes to find himself in each thought
That is as loud as a metal plate falling to the ground
In the burning hell where embers become coal
I hope to find my will, and a way out of the shackles
That make me feel like an imposter.

ABOUT THE POEM
"The poem basically describes what I feel like sometimes when I voice all the things I struggle with through poetry, but at the same time when I write poetry I tend to doubt the work I create, and it's a feeling that always fights to stay, the feeling of never being good enough or achieving enough. A feeling that you are just not as good as you think you are."

DOUBT

I run, it walks
Uncountable steps
Underneath
These heavy eyes.
I mime, it talks
Its voice feasts
In the silent nights
When the questions
It asks screams
In the hot shower
Where I attempt to wash
Its claws off my wet skin.
I doubt it sees

How my flesh is wasting
My hope deflating
I doubt it sees
How It's always first
And I'm always last.

ABOUT THE POEM

"The poem describes how sometimes self-doubt creeps in different forms, in my case it creeps in as voices in my head when I shower in silence and all I hear are the thoughts falling with each droplet that covers my feet."

ABOUT COLLEN

Collen is a 24 year-old, poet, artist, and engineering student, based in Johannesburg, South Africa. His published work is as follows: *On the Edge & A Poet's prayer* published by AVBOB poetry; *Artist,* featured in *Letting in the light: A mental wellness anthology; Time*, a third placed poem on the AVBOB mini-poetry competition 2021; *When you chose to leave, Her, Death and These walls,* and a short story: *Trapped* published by Papers publishing(USA). *Under my skin, Our Love*, and *Grief* published by Poetry Potion. *Anchored roots* published by Notepad poetry.
Instagram: @Just_collen

Poetry by Sandra Noel

OCEAN PULL OF A WINTER DAWN

Sometimes, I heave my head down the slip,
the weights with no words;
twisted guilt in tar-dark heart.

Water's mist-breath ripples liquid corduroy
weaving soft fascination around my body.
Her green transparency cloaks my shoulders
and she takes me in her pull and glide,
pulsing the plausible.

When I re-earth,
I take only her salt-drops,
sea-memory of sun.

ABOUT THE POEM
"I wrote this poem to explore the benefits of sea swimming on my own mental health and how it helps me day to day when close and dear people are suffering."

SEND A NOTE BACK FOR THE LOW DAYS

Those pink triangles
Mum swallows on the hopeless days
when you tip-toe on the chair,
reach into the larder
behind the *hundreds and thousands.*
Tip one into the cap,
place in her left hand
and watch the fog
take her to Valium sofa.

Her record player,
your needle stuck in her groove;
know that forty years on
her string will pull still.
When you find the slippers
she thinks were stolen,
fix the remote, dripping tap,

the foreboding wind;

know it never was your fault.

ABOUT THE POEM
"I wrote this to explore my feelings around my mother's mental health over the years and the impact it had on me as a teenager and our relationship."

GRASPING

her shudder-breaths tune
to feet across the landing
proof of scraping through each tar-dark night

she won't tell how her tears
soak the pillow slips
with wakeful night mountains of worry

the act of balancing
at the top of the chasm
to lean in so far yet not too much

ABOUT THE POEM
"I wrote this poem to explore the helplessness felt when a loved one is suffering."

JEAN'S CHECKING FOR STARS THROUGH THE SUNNY WINDOW

She's twinkling with multi versions of herself,
prisms of snow-hair blurring her edges.

I need you, she says to the doll with the scared eyes,
sitting in the window across the patio.
You must be with me,
shame my family couldn't make it.

I'm here, I say,
bigging up the best scampi and chip dinner
for the best mum.

She flies back in through the closed window.
I don't like scampi,

you must take me with you.

ABOUT THE POEM
"I wrote this poem to explore the effect of my mother's dementia, and what has and hasn't changed in our relationship since her diagnosis."

ABOUT SANDRA
Sandra is a poet from Jersey, Channel Islands, who enjoys writing about the ordinary in unusual ways. Her passion for sea swimming for mental health stability, and her love of nature, weaves its way through much of her work. Sandra's poetry appears in *The Phare, Flights, Black Nore, Yaffle, Indigo Dreams, The Ekphrastic Review, The Lake* and others. She has poems on Guernsey buses, and is highly commended in the Yaffle competition 2023. Sandra is working on her first collection.

Poetry by Tinamarie Cox

SHARING MY INSOMNIA WITH A DEMON

I wanted to burn a hole in my arm
but instead, I wrote poetry.

I was restless and tired and lonely,
a potent mixed drink late at night.

The intoxicating brew swirled around my skull
like the rounded bone was a tulip glass,
blending sticky ideas and harmful flavors.

A demon appeared on my shoulder,
called forth by the spell of my dark thoughts,
and shared terrible dreams with me.

"Less messy," he said in my ear
with burning matches in his eyes,
when I started thinking about red ribbons feeling silky.

He had chased away the angel, his counterweight.
Or maybe the heavenly being had just stayed asleep
and didn't rise in the middle of the night with us.

Without a little winged creature in white,
there was no balancing the demon's gravity.
No arguments against his suggestions.
Nothing holding me up.

Or holding me back.

So, I held myself.
Gritted my teeth while the demon continued to speak.

I did my best to ignore his persuasive tongue,
and smother the fires on his fingertips.

I managed to free a single tear.

His strength came out with my salt
and his power trickled down my cheek.

The battle wasn't won,
but I managed a stalemate.

The demon went on to live,
to tempt me another night.

And I continue to write about him,
my verses keep him at bay.

ABOUT THE POEM
"I think this poem is fairly self-explanatory. I literally wrote it to distract myself from a self-harm attempt late one night. I have struggled with depression, anxiety, suicide and self-harm ideation for most of my life. The night hours tend to be the hardest for me when I am circling through a depressive episode. In my insomnia, my mind spins and it's hard to stop myself from entertaining darker thoughts. A lot of my poetry is mental health related, but this one is one of the more obvious pieces."

ABOUT TINAMARIE
Tinamarie lives in Arizona, USA, with her husband and two children. Her written and visual work has appeared in several publications in a range of genres. She is also the author of a poetry chapbook, *Self-Destruction in Small Doses* (Bottlecap Press).
W: www.tinamariethinkstoomuch.weebly.com
FB: @tinamariethinkstoomuch
Instagram: @tinamariethinkstoomuch
Twitter (X): @tinamarie_cox

Poetry by Sheryl L. Fuller

DIAMOND CHILD

Oh, Oh, Diamond Child
I try to follow, but you're oh so wild
You flash away, with your infused style
I sit in awe, and I stay for a while

Multi-facets with little to say
Naturally take my breath away
Clarity in the light of the day
I move closer, and you shine anyway

That brilliance makes one feel free
I pulled the solitaire closer to me
I looked deeper for something to be
But The Diamond Child shines too bright to see

Dance and play, one of a kind
I look away, but you still shine
Precious, radiant, masterful you
Diamond Child is your love true?

I went looking for a Diamond Child
Gleaming light, perfectly wild
Clearly brilliant raw and rare to find,
Diamond Child never saw, the love left behind

Dance and play, one of a kind
I look away, but you still shine
Precious, radiant, masterful you
Diamond Child is your love true?

PRETTY BUTTERFLY

It's nineteen hundred and twenty two miles to Memphis
I saw you on the street before I left
You were holding hands with your next victim
as the cosmic signal of my life reset

The truck drivers, nod, as I pass their lane
The wipers, rhythm, play a song of my pain

and I am alone, with thoughts that remain
of you and I, ... My pretty butterfly

Life is fancy for you, as you go
I tried to be fancy too. but you wouldn't stay
An opportunity came, for me to grow
The right thing to do, now I'm on my way

Crossing gates go down, all the twinkling lights
The bells ringing sound, echoing my plight
I'm sorry, for the one, stuck with you, tonight
Freight cars click by, ...My pretty butterfly

I gave it all my all, I really tried
I believed your words, all a lie
I needed that call, to save my pride
My thoughts a blur, I've almost arrived

Old highway, signs, behind the trees
Abandoned auto's, in the scenery
Heading now, for Tenn- e- ssee
Bye and bye, ... My pretty butterfly

Heading now, for Tenn- e- ssee
 Bye and bye, ... My pretty butterfly

ABOUT SHERYL
Sheryl is a writer, singer songwriter, and performing artist from
Chicago, USA. Sheryl's writing is inspired from her many life
experiences.
E: playnicekids@comcast.net

Poetry by S. D. Kilmer

LOOK AT ME

Don't you look at me.
It's so plain to see.
There's so much.
I'm not the person I want to be.

The past has been so cruel.
There has never been a school
To learn how to be human.
The Creator must of thought
that should have been natural.
As humans we simply fought
against our original nature, not so admirable.

What now shall we ...
What now shall I do?
How shall this life I construed
Change, transform, transcend
For the better?
To be less fettered.

I am the aggregate of all of them
who have interacted with me
and I with them.
Some for good.
Some poorly impacted.
Some not doing as they should.
Others like they're tuned in to the Creator.
Formation of the person, an arbitrator
of all those interactions.

Benefactions, microtransactions, overreactions,
counteractions, communal celebration, everyone
appreciation.
That's it! It takes all of us.
If we can just discuss, without a fuss.
All of us together being good to each other.
Being the best of ourselves shall surely delve
into the best of humanity.
When we live in a dynamic society.
Each of us are benefited

when all of us are committed
to Be
the best we can Be.

C'mon, look at me now.
You'd be pleased to see.
The new you!
The new me!

First appeared in *S. D. Kilmer's Existential Life* eJournal.

ABOUT THE POEM
"This poem traverses search for one's identity, through the dilemma with others, finally arriving to Self as the aggregate of one's choices and interactions with others."

FEAR OF THE MARKET PLACE

Grew up in a space without any love.
Prepared me not for the world.
Home was more like a Roman arena.
I was never prepared to deal
        with a life with the lions, the mad

men in suits and
uniforms, those who would
        steal my heart and soul.
Home would only teach me angst and fear.
Fear of the marketplace.

ABOUT THE POEM
"Adolescent angst in the face of a life in the world outside the childhood home."

THE HUMAN GAME

It's not me, it's all you.
I haven't a clue
How to play the human game.
What? Are we all suppos'd to be the same?
It all sounds pretty lame.

Go away, you're just too much.
I'm drowning in your affections.

I know you're not doing anything.
it's my own afflictions.
You are my everything.
I know that I am nothing
'Coz now no one knows me.
I might not even know my Self.
Doctor, can you give me one off the shelf?

The telly is burning.
I'm not even watching,
the way my life is turning.
Let's see how we're matching.
Go away now!
I've missed you so and how!

Let's lay in bed all day.
The world is so boring.
Or maybe I've just lost my way.
Looks to me, the world is so whoring.
Words are sometimes hard to say.

On the dole without any dough
I can still gets a rise from moments of
          detachment.
Since I can't always buy,
Into the supermarket abundance.
Yet stamps has never stomped out
hunger or poverty.

I wanna get back to the start
To try it all over.
Hoping wisdom hovers.

Strangers always treat me like I'm not acceptable,
          never beautiful. Rarely anyone's friend.
Enough reason to consider the end?

It's not for me, it's all for you.
I haven't a clue
How to play the human game.
What? Are we all suppos'd to be the same?
Hypocrisy, judgementalism, backstabbing.
It all sounds pretty lame.
Don't expect me to play
this human game.

ABOUT THE POEM
"This poem presents the ambiguity towards an impersonal Society while reflecting some symptoms of illness."

ABOUT S.D. KILMER
Symon is a Survivor of Child Adoption and related Child Abuse. Diagnosed in 1999 with Fibromyalgia, Systemic Depression and ADD. While employed at the local State Psychiatric hospital he was injured sustaining further skeletal-muscular problems. Music, poetry spirituality became a comfort and healing powers for Simon. His first poem written at age 11 entitled, *Look At Mine* about encouraging a potential love interest to consider him over the boy who is more obvious and popular choice. He holds a Certificate in Jewish Studies and a certificate in Conflict Resolution from Syracuse University. In 1993 received a New York State Court certified training in Mediation of Conflict leading him to practice Community & Family Mediation. Also holds a certificate of Training in Pastoral Care (1995) from the AAPC certified "Clergy Training Program in Pastoral Care" at the (since defunct) Onondaga Pastoral Counseling Center, in Syracuse, N.Y. Lastly, he holds a Bachelors of Professional Studies [B.P.S. 1998] degree in Orthodox Psychology & Conflict Resolution from State University of New York at Empire State College. Due to physical disabilities and financial deficiency, his pursuit of a Psy.D. degree and certification in Counseling became out of the question. He practiced Community & Family Mediation under supervision of the New Justice Conflict Resolution Services agency in Syracuse, N.Y. As well as, direct service of Pastoral Care & Orthodox Psychotherapy in Syracuse N.Y. under the aegis of the Orthodox Church. Symon continues to reside in his hometown in Central New York State, writing poetry through which he voices the adoptee experience and the salvific Faith & Lifestyle of the Orthodox Christian Community.
W: www.SDKilmer.com

Poetry by Nivedita Roy

HAMMER AND SEAL

Drenched in sweat he entered the premises
A bag full of tools to tackle the problems
The leaking tap, the blocked drain
His hands reveal the nerves strained
He knows which knob to knock
He knows how to tighten the screw
As I watch him deftly work his way
I ponder upon a million things
 My thoughts do sway
My sobbing heart beats, scars ooze too
Is there a glue to fight away my blues?
Does he have a key to tighten the leaks in my eyes ?
Wish he hammered away the throbbing ache which I hide
Would he be able to seal the pierced heart ?
Why don't the noisy tools drown the sharp tongues echoing in my
ears ?
Wishing away my aches
Wiping away my tears
I count the cash due towards the repairs
The taps and pipes in my house
Are now good as new
The plumber has sealed the leaks
Here my tears and aches begin to peak
A tepid tea, a diary, and my glasses
Are my tools to seal the rough patches

ABOUT THE POEM
*"I wrote this poem while I was overwhelmed with job responsibilities,
crazily worried about my mother and her loneliness - who lives in
India - hopelessness and loneliness, to say the least. It was taking its
toll on my mental health. I was going through bouts of anger issues
and moodiness. Writing has been cathartic too, as I have suffered the
loss of my younger brother and father within a gap of eight years."*

Poetry by Pallavi Jain

LONELINESS

So many people are around me
And so much noise around
Even in a crowd I'm alone
This is the burden of loneliness
I am tired of carrying
I am battling
alone all the time
The sound of void
pierces my ears
The mask that I am wearing of happiness
It's hollow from inside
My voice comes crashing back
through stone walls
The noise is inside me
If I loose myself in the fair of the world
May be i can find me
I just wanted
Someone to sit with me for some time
someone to hold my hand
Look into my eyes
And be with me
My heart is like water
It is becoming numb
How I wish
Someone would laugh with me
Listen to me and
Pour one's heart
May be than the rust of loneliness
Wouldn't consume my heart.

NO ONE CAN PLAY YOUR PART

A piece of my candle stand broke
I fixed it with glue
It did take some time
I fixed it
It lights up my room just as fine
Show me the broken piece of your heart
We ll fix it together

I need you
As no one can play your part

In summer's scorching heat
My plant started to shrivel
I nurtured it to life
It's okay if you shrivel
Give me a chance
I will be with you
We will find some way
As no one can play your part

Let us be there for each other
Whether it's day or night
Summer or winter
Let us share happiness and sorrow
Ups and down
I may not show
But I need you
As no one can play your part

ABOUT PALLAVI
Pallavi (MSc and M. Phil in chemistry) lives in Bahrain. She is an artist and bilingual writer originally from India. She is self taught, and enjoys exploring various art forms and mediums.
Instagram: @bhoomi_our_land

Poetry by Rachel M. Clark

STILL I FALL

Each morning is a resurrection—
pulling myself from the quicksand
that has refilled the hole inside.

Some days I can get all the way out
and walk about freely—
passersby would never guess.

Other days I get as far as my elbows
and brace myself on the edge,
breathing like a stranded fish,
gills working furiously.

There are those who say this ritual
will soften with time-discipline-love.
Perhaps they are right—

they do not speak from empyrean heights,
but their chorus stands in a major key
and mine is pitched in the relative minor.

I am an apostle of melancholy
returning home each night
from the breezy-sunny-lighter perches
to the dark, close caverns of despair.

HAPPINESS

Oh to shake off the downbeat of shame
and rise up
like a dandelion seed blown into the air
with all its dancing cousins.

Oh to banish life's sad tuning—
like a tear that is sudden-dried
at its source by something
more beautiful than sorrow.

What is that something—

it is ten thousand somethings—
each one lobbying the seer
to be seen.

It is a choice to tie one's soul
to the wind, marking
each new uplift, like a
knot on a kite string. So long.

UNARMED

Bottled emotions do not age well.
Until we befriend our fears
our tender feelings turn
sour and corrosive: a violent vintage.

This is the way of villains and victims.
There is another way. The way of love.
Unarmed, our greatest weakness
becomes our greatest strength.

Accepting this unlikely truth,
everything else falls away.
There is nothing left to remove
or cling to or control. We are free.

ABOUT THE POEMS
*"These three, short lyric poems trace the poet's personal journey
from mental unwellness to greater mental health. The first, 'Still I
Fall' is an ironic salute to 'Still I Rise' by Maya Angelou, in which the
poet is struggling to be "up" while her nature and nurture pull her
down. In the second, 'Happiness', the poet is choosing to let the
persistent beauty of the world uplift her. The third, 'Unarmed' is a
more prosaic explication of the work we must do to stay emotionally
healthy."*

ABOUT RACHEL
Rachel received a BA in Drama from Bennington College, and an MDiv
from San Francisco Theological Seminary. While raising her children,
she directed educational programs in several churches, and worked
as an actor and acting teacher. She and her husband live in Falls
Church, Virginia, USA, where she tutors ESOL students for the local
literacy council and leads a small poetry salon on Zoom.

Poetry by Dr. Tamali Neogi

LIGHTED PLATEAU

I have been walking and walking for years
To reach Light, to feel it, to bathe in it
Ever since the night I had the dream
Hand in hand, the angels form a chain,
Someone says, they are celebrating the birth of a special child,
Encircling light. Yes I was a pregnant woman then.
Though tried much to see over their shoulders, I couldn't,
Light, what is your colour, what is your shape, how are you?
I was not allowed to know.

Walking and walking
Alas! Hers is a world where no morning sky greets the little soul
awake from sleep,
A zone of rainy evenings, followed by long, painful nights, never
ending.
An ailing child turns violent. Traumatic.
The mother awaits Light,
Walking and walking since the day she sits by the window to breathe
fresh air,
And the silhouettes of trees against the evening sky
Appear to her as if characters from the past,
Buried in deep, silenced by easy lapses and kind forgetfulness.
Soon they start speaking to her.
On her evening walks, she hears their whispers
"Soon you will reach the field flooded by Light where the angels
dance".

Every minute soaked in high patience and deep love,
The child grows up
Reading her poems.
Flashing through his mindscape the hopes of a lighted plateau,
Soon he will teach the habitants of that blighted world,
If you don't see Light, be it yourself.
Else, walk and walk. Live in hope.

ABOUT TAMALI
Tamali is Assistant Professor in department of English, Gushkara
College (Affiliated to the University of Burdwan), West Bengal, India.
A Gold Medallist alumni of the University of Burdwan, she has
authored *Woman of Patashpur* and presented/published more than a

dozen research papers/reviews in UGC CARE and WEB of SCIENCE journals during her eighteen year teaching career. She has authored the book titled *V.S. Naipaul's Dark and Comic Vision*, (Authorspress, New Delhi, 2023). She is the editor of *Postmodern Voices, Volume Viii,* (Earth Vision Publication, 2022). She is the associate editor of *An Anthology of Ethical Poetry*. Her poems and research articles are translated into Chinese and Romanian languages.

Poetry by Miroslava Panayotova

THE WALL

Everything is so common and simple!
You only need to close your eyes
and forget your dreams,
put out the lights under your eyelids.
You have to forget the music,
the greenery in the rain,
the rain splash and the cold,
which tells you that you are still
what you are.
You have to close your eyes and smile,
smile at the rain, which is no longer rain,
smile at the grass, which is not grass,
smile at the smile that isn't a smile anymore.
The lamps go out into pre-morning twilight.
The street is scary, I'm afraid of the street.
The good is well chewed and weighed,
with a price tag!
Look, on the other side
they sell the good more expensive!
The wall is waiting for you,
the deaf wall is waiting for you.
Will you catch the fog,
will you catch the lie, long and nasty,
well oiled,
with interposed teeth?

White bouquets?
I'll overwhelm you with them.
I stripped the trees,
I picked chestnuts,
I will shave my head
and will cover it with chestnuts
to have brown hair which I have without it!
I will drink water
from the fountain in the garden
but before I take a sip,
I'll stop for a while
to hear the gush and grasp the meaning
of the coming sip
and the green leaves above me,

forming a broad-brimmed hat.
In the evening that comes,
I'll look at the branches until I get frozen
and call the dog - just to see it.

ABOUT THE POEM
"This poem was written in the '70s. I had experienced personal disappointments and was very close to depression. Fortunately, this period has passed, but even now, because I am very sensitive, I guard against negative emotions."

ABOUT MIROSLAVA
Miroslava graduated from Plovdiv University, speciality Bulgarian philology and English language. She has published poems, stories, tales, aphorisms, essays, criticisms, translations, articles and interviews, as well as a large number of books, and her verses have been translated into English, Spanish, Greek, Albenian and Uzbek.

Poetry by Holly Dowds

THE BED IS RED

which would never be my choice.
No, I'd never choose a red bed.
But look, none of this is my choice:
lying flat on my back with chains circling my chest,
my waist, my shins.

Where am I? I'm just floating in a white space.
No floors, no doors, no walls or windows.
Well, this makes me very sleepy.
I'll just drift off to sleep.
Sleeping, sleeping, sleeping.

And that's what I did again and again that first day.
For some reason I was able to get out of bed to feed the cat,
use the toilet. Then back to the chains,
upon the bed that is red.
Sleeping, sleeping, sleeping.

The second day was the same as the first,
escaping only for the toilet and the cat.
Then back in chains not even able to go for food.
White space, red bed and chains.
Sleeping, sleeping, sleeping.

The third day was the same until something told me
I could call my son.
He arrived and I was back in the real world,
the everyone world.
A trip to the E.R. ensued,
then an ambulance ride to the mental ward.

No matter, because I was back in the real world,
the everyone world.
The staff fed me, poked and prodded me,
finally drugged me.
Back to sleep, sweet sleep.

Five days later of new medicine
had me arguing
that I was well enough to leave.

On day six I was released, following this conversation
with my new doctor:

Will this happen to me again?
      No, not likely because your body on the meds
      reacted quickly and effectively against your
      psychotic break.
So, I'll be OK?
Well, you'll never be the same person again.

ABOUT THE POEM
"This poem describes my psychotic break."

I WOULD LIKE TO EXPLAIN

          to that boy doctor,
the one who said You probably
have dysthymia; *DEPRESSION,*
who saw my eyebrows bunch
so then he said
As I understand it,
that means feeling as if
you are about to fall into a big hole

          to that boy doctor
to whom I wanted to yell
NO - it's like you are searching
in your flooding backyard,
looking for something important
and you wonder how long you have
before the water reaches the electrical panel
THAT'S how it feels

          but I was younger then
so now I would say
It's like you are a fish
in a dead sea
where no smaller fish
are living
not even algae
so the only things to eat
are the worms on hooks

          and now I would add

I aspire to be the fish who thieves the worms.

ABOUT THE POEM
"This poem shows my progression through several years of increasingly overcoming severe depression."

AT DEATH'S DOOR

You were a stagehand full of strife,
trying to cue all the lines of my life.
Your black scythe beckoned me to suicide.
All my strength used; I followed my own guide.

All those years, all those tears, how could I forget
the decades spent resisting your net?
But now you have no choice but to succumb,
because I have won. Forever I have won.

That's why I'm dancin' and prancin' at Death's door,
'cause I'm not afraid of you no more, no more.

You used my chemistry, my own story,
to support your supposed glory.
But you will not get me, not by my own hand.
I've taken my life back. I am in command.

That's why I'm dancin' and prancin' at Death's door,
'cause I'm not afraid of you no more, no more.

ABOUT THE POEM
"This poem celebrates my victory over severe depression, which led me to consider suicide."

ABOUT HOLLY
Holly is a survivor of both acute depressions and a psychotic break. She credits the act of poetry writing as part of her cure. She has been published in a half-dozen literary magazines and co-authored two books.
E: hollydowdspoet@gmail.com

Poetry by Judy DeCroce

I CAN SEE CLEARLY NOW

You never feared shadows or,
spoke of falling days
cold, iced over.

The wind turned...turns.
It was morning or dusk...
when you walked past the moment

that was the center of your life.
Now, clouds mesh and
snow hills your shoulders.

Something has darkened.
You see it there
closer...
an ending,

and approach.

ABOUT JUDY
Judy is an internationally published poet, flash fiction writer, and recently published *The Posture Of Trees*, a book of poetry with her husband, Antoni Ooto. Her poem, *One Woman Leads to Another*, was nominated for the Pushcart Prize. She is also a professional storyteller, and teacher of that genre, as well as offering courses in flash fiction. She lives in rural upstate New York, USA.
LinkedIn:@ @JudyDeCroce

Poetry by Molly Forrester

CHOICES

The cracks in the foundation started long ago,
Choices made, as nurturing fades, and slowly turns to stone.
A wall built up over time,
Confusion abounds, because I thought you were mine.

Witnessing you leaving,
I asked myself and God, please tell me something worth believing.
The cracks deepened,
My troubled heart had no fight left, and the unloving seeped in.

Did you turn your back because of something I did, or something I am?
This can't be the universe's master plan.
Followed your lead and turned my back as well,
If you hate me then I'll hate me too, and I'll do it really well.

I learned about wanting, what a futile exercise,
The cracks became wide, as fear and anger intertwined.
Yearning quietly for what was supposed to belong to me,
But by your choices, we were hopelessly unfree.

Be my safety, I pleaded endlessly,
But a turned back could neither give nor receive.

ABOUT THE POEM
"This poem discusses childhood neglect, abandonment, and the revolving door of a drug-addicted parent."

TRIGGER WARNING

They say "trigger warning" but my triggers are everything and nothing at the same time.
It's like building your dream house on an unsteady foundation and saying "it's fine."
It's like going to a movie and realizing you've been that villain your whole life.
It's like laughing, swinging from tree to tree and then getting caught up in vines.
I try, and I try, and I try, I push and I pull, but the flood, it's

inevitable.
By the time I realize I'm drowning in the irrational, all the life rafts are full.
Triggered, I am, for the pain and suffering is what I live and breathe;
I heed your warning, but for me there is no reprieve.

ABOUT THE POEM
"This poem discusses feeling victim to mental health triggers which are often intrusive and unwanted."

MORE GRAY DAYS

The amusement park ride whips and whirls,
As if by my own force,
I can see myself, hear myself,
Floating above, but I can't alter the course.

"She's crazy," they say,
"Such a loser," they chant,
I try to find the part that can fight back,
But I can't.

I need more gray days,
Not a rhythm of black then white, then black again,
Ironically, my core is made up of black and white,
But only one by name and skin.

I need more gray days;
I yearn for a certain longevity to my optimism.
No more uncontrollable flights up to la-la-land,
And inevitable crashes to catastrophism.

ABOUT THE POEM
"This poem discusses the rollercoaster of emotions I experience suffering from Borderline Personality Disorder and PTSD."

ABOUT MOLLY
Molly is a 32 year-old novice poet, based in Massachusetts, USA, who hopes to help people feel seen and understood through the honesty and rawness of her creative reflections. She has not been published previously, and is currently a stay-at-home mom to her 2 year-old son. Her work takes a deep dive into the struggles and realities of single motherhood, depression, anxiety, PTSD, childhood trauma, sexual abuse, and Borderline Personality Disorder. *"I started writing*

as a process of excavating parts of me that had been buried and unidentified for many years. I use writing as a stream of consciousness exercise which helps me process past traumatic experiences and find compassion for my resulting mental health struggles. Instead of being scared of my pain, I have given it purpose through creative expression. Poetry acts as a direct portal to my internal dialogue, so my work often hits in an honest and reflective way. Letting my words flow out naturally and embracing vulnerability makes me feel empowered and more in control of my story."

Poetry by Katherine Brownlie

KNOWING

Nothing has changed
but everything is different
connaissance whispering
can unfold all that has
gone before
and although I acted as
though I knew
to hear those words out loud
defining and forming the
new reality
which can never be typical
it saddens me to the depths
and feels for you
for all those misunderstandings
and reasons why which
never were yours
I saw through my eyes
but yours I cannot now tell
I am unsure to pry
the paradigm shift
is the more odd as
the content of the world
appears to be familiar
as realisation falls
like leaves raining down
a contrite abscission
tipping and rolling
melting to the ground
revealing the bare truth
where life just carries on
imperfectly.

ABOUT KATHERINE
Katherine is a British poet currently living in France. Her poetry is
concerned with human, other species and environmental inter-
connectivity. The social and cultural pressures which affect us all
means that we are constantly under subliminal attack. However, this
poem speaks with the imperfect voice of an empath, and forms a
path to an awakening of sorts.

Poetry by Cristín Mann

I THINK I NEED TO GET HELP

Our eyes meet and he nods.
I am at the kitchen table, head in hands.
He has just returned with our daughter,
asleep in his arms.

He followed on later, I travelled alone.
I could not stay there any longer.
I considered swerving into the oncoming traffic, but I didn't,
Because of the little girl in the patent blue shoes.

They decided to go boating. I stayed behind,
Nursing my shame in the dark.
Jealousy foamed at the brutal unfairness,
Their heedless good fortune, our chasm of loss.

We were given the single room.
Just space for a small double and a cot.
The families took the family rooms, of course.
We split the bill.

Just the one then?' they'd asked, the evening before.
'Lucky you! My three are always at war!'
'Yes, one little girl', talon clawed at my throat,
Silent shriek burning holes in my stomach.

I finally managed to leave the bathroom,
To make my way down the stairs,
I tried to sneak past the kitchen, but they saw me and pounced,
'Where've you been?'
My face burned.

Cousins laugh in the sun, Aunts and Uncles look on.
Trapped in the Airbnb bathroom, I scrub my teeth hard.
Their laughter pierces my flesh, charred insides exposed.
Entrails for greedy, chattering crows to pick over.

I think I need to get help.

ABOUT THE POEM
"This one was about the moment at a friend's 40th birthday weekend when I realised that I was not 'OK'."

NOT CARVED IN STONE

As far back as I can remember,
I have been on the outside, looking in.
Whispered intimacy, cool girls having fun,
I gazed hungrily, from afar.

Watchful eyes peering through
Hospital glass.
Blotchy cheeks waiting at the
Line in the grass.

Too clever, too shy, too other,
And all the while desperate to please.
I walked alone in the park,
My feet beginning to freeze.

I got older; it helped.
I got braver, found love.
I was not inside, not yet,
But I felt less apart.

Then, the sucker punch,
'Unable to naturally conceive'.
Thorns smothered my body,
Burrowed deep into my bones.

Somehow, we still made a baby,
Crazy science, crazier luck.
High on gas and oxytocin,
We held tight to our beautiful child.

Next, we tried for a sibling,
So our daughter would not be alone.
We tried so hard, too hard,
But his time, our luck did not hold.

No second blue line,
No double buggy for walks,
No John Lewis bunk beds,

We were outside once more.

Would she be excluded too?
An only child facing the world.
Would she be enough for 'them'?
Would they let her take part?

Enough!
This circle does not have to repeat.
I can choose an untrodden path,
For my child,
For myself.

Let her be her.
(Let me be me).
Let her live, love and grow,
Accepted and seen.

Let her not have to choose
Between outside and in,
Between 'them' and 'us',
Let her simply be free.

We are not carved in stone.

ABOUT THE POEM
"This one is about my persistent feelings of 'otherness' and rejection for most of my life, which I think were the roots of my periodic anxiety and depression from teenage years on ... But it's mostly about my fear of passing this on to my beautiful daughter, and my relief in realising that we don't have to continue to circle the past. We can move forward, with the right help."

RAGDOLL

Slumped forward she sits,
Glass-eyed and cold.
No life left in the old girl.
Her best days long gone.

She remembers the good days,
The music, the laughs.
She forgets the pain,
The heartache, rejections.

Days when the rules were harsh,
But at least they were clear.
When family felt simple,
Not a maze of wrong turns.

You gaze upon her with distaste.

So flawed...
Experienced.
So weak...
Kind.
Skin that sags...
With truth.
Cast adrift...
Coming home.

Embrace her,
Accept her,
Love her.
She is you.

ABOUT THE POEM

"This one was written following a therapy session where the therapist got me to use props to help me understand how I was feeling about myself and my immediate family members. It was an immensely powerful and healing experience that I still vividly remember, 11 years later."

ABOUT CRISTÍN

Cristín is a poet based in Lismore, Co. Waterford, Republic of Ireland. She began writing in 2012, after a period of intense personal trauma, which culminated in a breakdown. She initially used writing as therapy - a way of getting the bile and fears out of her head and gaining perspective on and ultimately some control over her thoughts and reactions. Over time, as Cristín began to heal (not that this journey is ever complete), she discovered that poetry is not only amazing therapy for oneself, but also a source of joy and satisfaction, when shared with others. She is now part of the wonderfully supportive West Waterford Writers Group, has taken part in multiple spoken word poetry workshops run by Chris Redmond of Tongue Fu fame, and enjoys writing and performing her poetry, as often as she can. She feels very lucky to have found so much kindness and beauty in her life and to be able to appreciate it increasingly fully.

Poetry by Shalini Vaghjee

MAN ... STOP! ... BREATHE ...!

Deep down Man acquires
Wealth and possessions
to keep death at bay

Deep down man secures
Companions to keep
loneliness away

Deep down man clings
To technology and drugs
to keep rejection out of play.

Oppressed by doubt, waste, and emptiness,
Deep down a fight takes place
In the darkness of his soul.

Deep down, in this madness,
The fight perpetually rages.

Man ... stop! ... Breathe!

Turn your gaze within!

Are you brave enough
To stand up against tyranny and face pain?

Man ... stop!... Breathe!
Are you brave enough
To fight for what is right and even face death?

Man ... stop! ... Breathe!
Are you brave enough
To set aside the subtle whisperings of your lower self
And reveal your own authentic inspiration?

Man, stop! Breathe!
Are you brave enough
To face your true self?

Are you brave enough

To stand naked and alone

Without intermediaries and face your Creator?
Only faith and surrender can restore...
Harmony. Love. Peace.

Man
Stop
Breathe.

ABOUT THE POEM
"I wrote this poem as I was trying to find a way to deal with the madness which was the cause of all mental tensions in my house, as well as those of friends and acquaintances. In my life, being bedridden due to an incurable degenerative illness, I live my life one day at a time, one breath at a time. I feel that this could be the best start for anyone to keep their sanity as the world is a mad place."

THE LITTLE VOICE

Unexpected. Uninvited, Unforgiving It came,
and turned the whole world into a battlefield.

The rich, the poor,
From North to South
From East to West
No one is spared.
Death rates and critical cases are on the rise.
Though cancer is still the main killer
Doctors and big Pharma join hands in glee
"Let's find a cure, if not, a vaccine!"
Banks and businessmen join in.

Friends and family are depressed
The lady next door lost her job... another suicide.
Fear and insecurity run riot
People look up, down, left, right,
Their eyes are hollows of terror.
Loss of employment
Salary cuts
Higher cost of living
People are exploited, enslaved, used like machines.
Stress and depression are the new fashion.
Anxiousness and irritability shroud the mind

Hypertension and cardiovascular diseases take their toll on the drained psyche.
Layers of masks and lies are everywhere
On Instagram, Snapchat, Twitter, Facebook, Tik Tok, LinkedIn, WhatsApp, even the news.
The number of followers is the new benchmark
To get a job
Or a publisher.
Education is rotten.
Common sense is endangered
Stupidity has taken over the world.

Is the world doomed?
Is this a point of no return?
Or can it be saved?
In the darkness of this madness
The little voice cries out:
Why am I here?
What does this mean?
Where do I go?

The little voice cries out
For a true education embracing Livelihood, well-being and love.
Contemplating the secrets of life and death.
The little voice cries out
For a wholesome education
Where man, woman and society
Are healthy, loving and compassionate,
Humanity overflowing with joy
Always ready to share with anyone.
Where no-one is a stranger on earth.

ABOUT THE POEM
"This was written during the lockdown where everyone was stuck at home, I could not get my necessary treatments and it made me think: can something invisible and intangible stop the whole world: developed countries as well as underdeveloped ones. Kings, emperors, paupers, criminals as well as those who tread the righteous path were all affected. From my bed, I watched life unfolding this unforgiving mystery and wondered what could be the answer!"

ABOUT SHALINI
Originally from the island of Mauritius, but currently based in Bahrain, Shalini is a Civil Engineer with a post graduate degree in Project

Management. She is a member of Bahrain Writers Circle and has participated in Colours of Life and Confluence events for the past two years. She loves travelling, painting, writing, gardening, surfing and sharing her experiences. She also enjoys cooking and experimenting in the kitchen. However, due to health restrictions, her passions are now rather limited. However, she continues to be a seeker, and believes in enjoying whatever she can and longs for a utopian world where peace and joy prevails.

Donna Zephrine's story

Reflecting back on my life, my poor mental health was a cumulation of all life events: my mom being elderly and physically challenged; my sister assaulted me when she was drunk - I ended up having to get reconstructive surgery because I lost a piece of bone near my eye (orbital floor fracture - surgeon put in a steel plate); two soldiers in my unit got killed in Iraq; I met a Wounded Warriors Project veteran from Peer Support, he was doing his own peer support group in Long Island for veterans with mental health - I was supporting his cause for an event when he became unprofessional, we got in a disagreement and he banned me from the program; I experienced the loss of my father who died from colon cancer; I was married and then getting a divorce, and I lost my baby at 24 weeks - he only lived a day. Also, after I graduated high school at age 23, a former mentor of mine wanted something more than to be friends, and that was my first encounter of sexual trauma. When I joined the Army Reserves, I also experienced military sexual trauma from a senior ranking NCO, who touched me inappropriately and made inappropriate comments. My PTSD is with my war trauma - losing my squad leader and another soldier in my unit, as well as soldiers in my divisions who also lost their lives.

I also had learning disabilities when I was young too, which has had a significant impact on me throughout my entire life, and has meant that I have often been excluded from certain activities and events.

In the Military I spoke to my chaplain and the professional staff at Tuttle Army Clinic for mental health, and got a neuro psych test done at the facility. I was also given a referral to see a speech pathologist. I was then deployed to Iraq. After getting an honorable discharge, I returned to the US and registered at my VA Hospital in Northport NY.

The VA helped make a change in my recovery; with professional staff, as well as networking with other outside veterans organizations such as the Dwyer Peer Support, Team RWB, the veterans administration hospital, Heroes to Heroes, Team Red White and Blue, Team Rubicon and others. I have also faith in the Lord, and receive emotional and physical support by a number of spiritual advisors in organizations that are faith based.

I think the world perceives me as someone who learns things differently, and someone who does not easily understand, which means there are some people out there who want to take advantage of the situation. There are good people out in the world, but it is sometimes hard to find them. I perceive the world as having a majority of people who do not understand me. I have trust issues and do not trust many people. In my experiences people just talk and, when push comes to shove, there is generally no commitment.

To relieve stress, I try to exercise, like cycling and playing golf, as well as journaling and talking to professional staff at the Northport VA and Joseph Dwyer Project about my concerns and issues. They help me look at the situation objectively, and perhaps differently to how I see things. I also like listening to music, art therapy and writing poetry and narratives, and try to draft an outline of my thoughts by using visual images such as a vin diagram or mind map. I have a lot of mentors who have supported me too including Alan Jay Weissman, a New York State psychologist, who has been a mentor of mine for over 20 years. He has helped me a lot.

I try to be optimistic and take things one day at a time. I know life with mental health problems is not easy, but you have to think positively, and reach out to other people for help and guidance; you'll be amazed to find out there are people out there who would love to help a person in need. You meet all types of people, in walks of life, so do not let the negative people drain your goals and put you down. Life has taught me that in the eyes of adversity, believe in your dreams - it may take you a little longer than other people to get to them, but you can.

ABOUT DONNA
Donna was born in Harlem, New York. She graduated from Columbia University School of Social Work in May 2017, and currently works for the New York State Office of Mental Health at Pilgrim Psychiatric Center Outpatient Intensive Case Management as a Bridger. She is a combat veteran who completed two tours in Iraq. Since returning home Donna enjoys sharing her experiences and storytelling through writing and has been published internationally. Recently Donna took part in Warrior Chorus and Decruit which encourage self-expression through looking as classical literature and performing it while relating it to your own life with war and trauma. She is involved in World Team Sports, Veteran of Foreign Wars, Wounded Warrior Project and others, and serves on the advisory board of Heroes to Heroes.
FB: @donna.zephrine
Instagram: @donnazephrine
X: @dzephrine
LinkenIn: @donna-zephrine-3030063

Poetry by Siobhan Brownlie

TEARS OF JIYA

Do not give in to shoals of falling tears
For time will brighten your searing night
Content will be the friend of following years

A perverted father broke your frail frontiers
Harmed your body your mind and light
Do not give in to shoals of falling tears

A mother who should protect disappears
Cowardly she betrays maternal might
Content will be the friend of following years

In marital life brutal violence reappears
You struggled alone on a foreign site
Do not give in to shoals of falling tears

Family far away whose jealousy rears
Greedy and disregarding your plight
Content will be the friend of following years

Relinquish the hold of cruel flashbacks and fears
Be steady in new love and remain upright
Do not give in to shoals of falling tears
Content will be the friend of following years

A SONNET FOR LEON

I hardly know you Leon but I care
For we are linked by indirect blood
We both nourish a family leaf bud
So with these brief lines I will share
My thoughts on mute despair
When through a torrential flood
And left gasping on putrid mud
The mind is in an unbearable tear

Yet in yourself secretes a weapon
That can bolster sustain completely
Unsuspected ventures will beckon

Ridding yourself of dank history
Leon it's the moment to step in
To grasp youth's force and foresee

ABOUT THE POEMS
"These poems are addressed respectively to my daughter-in-law, Jiya, and to my son's half-brother, Leon. Both suffer from PTSD. I wrote the poems to support each of them. Jiya and Leon gave permission for the poems to be published with their names."

ABOUT SIOBHAN
Siobhan is a writer who is originally from New Zealand, and who lives in Le Mans, France. She is currently working on a collection of poems that covers experiences and history from her life span.

Poetry by Lisa Anderson

DOING THE DIRTY LAUNDRY

I brought him down
to wash away
every memory of him

In a basket is where he is
I throw every memory
of him into the
machine
I close the lid it
begins to fill
it starts to spin

Soak, rinse, churn,repeat
I try to cleanse him
from me with
the detergent
to erase him from me
forever

Washer done
I throw him into the
intense heat
of the Dryer
I am almost done
with him

Alarm goes off
the dryer is done
I did my dirty laundry
I rid myself
of him
in my memory

I fold with a
sense of peace
the clothes are
crisp and clean

One sock missing of course

ABOUT LISA

Lisa has belonged to two amazing writing groups for over five years. She feels that it is through her mental illness that she has found her writing voice. She has had her work in three anthologies, as well as, published her first book, a collection of haikus and poetry. She lives in Alberta, Canada.

Poetry by Pip McDonald

iOCD

The thought of contamination pulsates through my mind,
Perhaps this is compulsion by design,
The unwanted thoughts are like a persistent agitator,
If I don't clean now there'll be more work to do later,
There is never any peace with the OCD theatre and being onstage,
It is an obsessive performance trapped in a cage.

When will these thoughts ever cease?
The music of this condition is like a song that plays on repeat,
Perhaps I need to explore exposure,
In order to find some closure,
I hope that radical thinking will help me overcome this rift,
Perhaps my OCD is really a gift.

ABOUT THE POEM
"I have battled with OCD in various forms throughout my life. Poetry allows me to share my lived experience of managing (and not managing) the condition."

ABOUT PIP
Based in England, Pip is an experimental performance poet. She has recently performed at High Tide Festival in Twickenham and Wandsworth Fringe Festival. She has recently screened a poetry film at the 11th Annual City Lit Film and Animation Festival in London. She was the Poet-in-Residence at the Learning & Skills Research Network (LSRN) annual conference in Birmingham. She is currently working on her first book *Notorium*. She has published original poems in a range of poetry anthologies and online magazines.
Instagram: @pipmac6
Twitter (X): @pipmac6

Poetry by Peter Devonald

HEART OF ILLNESS, FLOWERS

My Mother could always cope with illness
she knew exactly what to say and do to help

but never with mental health issues, it didn't even
exist for her. She said she was never unhappy, ever.

If we were sad she'd fuss and put her hand to our forehead
You must be coming down with something? You are a bit hot.

And we'd take to our bed with all our sad thoughts and regrets
hot lemon drink and soup, lots of water, care and sympathy.

We'd fixate on what disease we had, convinced ourselves into illness
or just wondered what sickness would strike us down next.

Somehow illness and mental health combined
even more than they do in real life. Mind and body entwined

stress flares illness but sometimes depression stands alone.
Mum left us feeling ill every time we were depressed, no words left.

THE PAST JUST IS, TRUST ME

They lied
the truth doesn't always come out
the truth remains stubbornly buried
in a deep dark damp place, covered by shame.
We can focus on our healing all we want
the guilty are very rarely prosecuted, trust me.

They lied
live your best life is the greatest victory of all
that's the way to really beat them
to be happy, successful and kind.
Reality still eats away at us, the sore wound, throbbing
the innocent are always prosecuted, trust me.

They lied
be the better person and walk away, don't turn back

let the past be passed, bygones be bygones
live in the moment and feel blessed.
Nightmares don't allow that, quiet moments don't allow that
screaming shrieking shadows waiting, waiting, trust me.

They lied
they said, take care of your mental health
focus on the road ahead, be patient
day by day it will get easier, calmer and simpler.
Day by day will be another day away from what happened
the storm still rages, trust me.

They lied
to suggest that there is some sort of balance in the world
the burning desperate terrible injustice gnaws away
a parasite, a bloodsucker, right at the heart of us.
A leech, sucking marrow out of bone
cruelty stays with you, trust me.

They lied
they said be the better person, be the change
to hang on the past is to hang yourself
but yesterday doesn't change, history our forever friend
taunting, yearning, hoping, breaking, kissing
I try my best and will survive, trust me.

They lied
our perception doesn't stay the same, it's fluid
all our demons can be tamed, eventually
wrinkles of a life smoothed, one by one, softly.
Believe in tomorrow, survive, survive, thrive –
living the life you love is the perfect response, trust me.

ABOUT PETER
Peter is joint winner of FofHCS Poetry Award 2023, winner Waltham
Forest Poetry Competition 2022 and Heart Of Heatons Poetry Award
2021. His poems have been extensively published and has been
nominated for the Forward Prize: Best Single Poem. Poet in residence
at Haus-a-rest. As a screenwriter, winner of 50+ film awards, former
senior judge/mentor Peter Ustinov Awards (iemmys) and Children's
Bafta nominated.
W: www.scriptfirst.com
Instagram: @peterdevonald
FB: @pdevonald

Poetry by Francis Muzofa

WHY? BECAUSE

I
Looking back
From an ariel view
I view
I review
With clarity
With sobriety
With serenity
With sincerity
I see
I relate
It's a bit late
But listen to the late
Before it's too late

From heaven's balcony
I speak
Why did I
I took life
My own life
Coward you might say
Stupid you might say
Selfish you might say
But hear what I have to say
Because I never meant to sell fish

I was overwhelmed
I was engulfed—Gulf war
I carried the entire universe
On my two shoulders
I was lonely
I fought lone battles
In my days
In my sleeps
None understood me
None talked to me
None cared enough
None empathized
None sympathized
I wallowed

I cried
I yelled silently
All doors shut on me
The only door open
Was written Suicide
I entered that room

Check on family
Check on neighbor
Check on colleague
Watch out for signs and symptoms
Watch out for distress calls
Read stress
Read depression
Between life and death
Is a very thin line
Crossing over to death is easy
The reverse is impossible
Talk to her
Talk to him
I talked to myself
I lied to myself
Taking myself
Was silly

It's now very clear
With the benefit of Hindsight's eye
Do not enter the suicide room
It locks from outside
You won't come outside forever.

ABOUT THE POEM
"This is a sad poem I wrote in honor of my cousin who committed suicide a few years ago. I personified him as he speaks from heaven. Knowing him as I did, I tried to imagine what is going on in heaven as he reviews what happened. How the loved ones didn't check on him and see that something is wrong. How he regrets the move he took. How he wants to give advice to others not to follow suite. He is speaking from heaven's balcony. That was the muse behind this poem."

ABOUT FRANCIS
Francis (aka @Pope) is an internationally published Zimbabwean poet. His poems have been published by a number of international magazines and journals. Francis believe poetry is the silver bullet that

the world need to heal its wounds, especially mental health. If one can't find someone to talk to, the page can be very therapeutic - pour it out, on the page. You will amazed by the healing power of poetry.
Twitter (X): @MuzofaFrancis

Poetry by Sue Tebble

BI POLAR EXPRESS

Bi Polar Express, I'm going up
My brain's on fire, I've done the washing up
I can't think, I can't focus, I'm bordering insane
Don't mess with me, I'm high octane

I'm standing at the station
I'm about to board the train
A mystery tour to happiness?
Or Clinically Insane?

Bi Polar Express, I'm going down
I just don't want no one around
I hate myself to the highest degree
Me and Myself we don't agree

I'm Casy Jones on the runaway train
I'm the 30's heroine but I can't escape
I'm Ivor the engine running to those hills
My brains derailed. Don't give me no more pills

Bi Polar Express, life's a bumpy ride
Bi Polar Express, step inside
I'm standing on the station
I'm about to board the train
A mystery tour to happiness?
or clinically insane?

ABOUT THE POEM
"I wrote this song three years ago about my mental health, trying to put a twist on it and make light. I also find laughter a great healing tool."

ABOUT SUE
Sue is a songwriter and musician. She has ADHD and PTSD from rape trauma. She was sectioned at 21; her diagnosis was Manic Depression. She is now 55 and has many coping strategies in place for her mental health; mostly singing and playing music, but swimming and getting as much nature and calm into her days as she can. She started her own charity nearly 10 years ago to help people with mental health issues through music - as music has helped her

heal. Her charity is called Mind The Gap, and she runs several music sessions in Norwich, and at the hospital where she was once sectioned. She finds writing cathartic, and encourages others to do the same by taking their negative experience and turning it into a positive song. There is still a great stigma attached to mental health and through music, performance and openness she aims to smash that stigma.

W: www.mindthegapmusic.org

Natalie Peterson's story

For as long as I could remember, my mother always called me a 'psychey.' On hearing that, as a child, it really did mess me up and got me questioning my instincts, and it often made me shed tears. So when I had my first psychotic episode, it felt like my sanity was already cursed; its fate determined by my mother. My father was Jamaican and diagnosed schizophrenic, and I have inherited my father's schizophrenic traits. My mother experienced a difficult life with my father, and she often terrorized and held control over me too and, although she's my mother, I will always despise her for that. However, I still don't know the exact trigger leading to my first diagnosis of schizophrenia - childhood traumas perhaps; being targeted at school for being a dunce, for being the odd one out, the loner, the mentally deteriorated one ... when you have constant negativity thrown at you from people with arrogance and ignorance, it makes you more of a savage.

One moment I would be okay, the next I really felt something was literally pulling me down into a dark hole, with no sign of light. I had suicide contemplations, and mentally and physically I couldn't breathe. I felt trapped; I couldn't get away from it, or shake myself out of it. The walls of my room felt like they were closing in and crushing me. I was angry, paranoid, unhappy and withdrawn, and so scared. I had a lot of physical complaints too, and weighing just five stone, completely malnourished.

Finally I got sectioned to a psychiatric hospital.

I have been living with schizophrenia within the community now for eighteen years. It's very rare to find someone like me with this condition living within the community; it is very difficult to make friends - society is generally very negative towards people with mental health conditions, but I see everyday as a bigger step towards loving and looking out for myself, and I refuse to go back into hospital. Life is exhausting though and very challenging. I try not to put my trust in people, and distance myself from them, as they almost always let me down and stab me in the back. And if I ever leave my guard down, it means I am more open to risk; society is evil - I don't know the last time I came across someone decent, solid and wholesome. So I am always on alert.

I know everyone's recovery is different, but medication has always been the key to my recovery, and the key to me being able to have lived in the community for as long as I have. And I believe people who do *not* take their prescribed medication should be kept in hospital - they should *not* be out on the pavements, a threat to society with their deranged behaviours, endangering themselves and others.

And since I've started to stand on my own two feet, creativity has played a big part in my lifestyle too - whether it's getting my hands covered in glue, or just mixing paints.

But I often think back and wonder if things were different with my family, what other possibilities in life would there be out there for me? But mud sticks ...

ABOUT NATALIE

Natalie's is of African heritage and lives in the UK. Her hobbies are travelling around London, listening to different genres of music, shopping for textiles, cooking, writing poetry, entering writing and art contests - just about anything creative.

Poetry by Stephen Kingsnorth

GREEN ROOM

As comfort, night time malted drink,
a pattern followed, by the clock,
without good reason to disown -
why would I end the day alone?

I'm told that change is all around,
I'm not an island to myself,
or I'll be simply left behind,
which is my lot - as I remind.
Change marks growth, from seed to bloom,
but do core values yet remain,
the mannerisms, polite style,
courtesy, respect, second mile?

While yes, there's much so strange to me,
it is routine, my leading star,
for I need anchor, taking strain,
secure hold, less their binding chain.
They have my ways mechanical,
when customary more my frame;
I sense my five alone will guide,
but well-worn paths from synapse hide?

Now dado, carpets, green I see;
this path I'm sure goes to my room.
But when the bell chimes in my head,
the corridors are meat and bread.
So here I am at bed and board,
with folks uncertain who they are;
that night time malted drink my own,
so I'll not end this day alone.

THERE

We really should have read the signs:
the glass paned door, like afterthought,
the rare-used tarmac covered path
the corridor from A to B,
for those intent on getting there.

The Sister took us,
a warder to defend her cause,
too much gabble, knowing all,
compassion as a gossamer.

We lapped it up as puppies might,
for She was god-like, trusted here,
and we of other disciplines,
not rude enough as others, right.

Mum gobbled at our offered sponge,
her blistered tongue dehydrate clue,
but, unattuned to obvious,
we trusted Trust, as taught to do,
for She mature, blue uniformed.

I dare not let my mind go there -
this verse creeps twenty five years on -
that dark place where our mother's care
was in the hands of hurried staff,
the nurse we should have harried there -
removed her from those clutches, dare
to bring her home with us, there, then.

I look back, incredulity,
but no one questioned medics then;
though shocked, but trained in courtesy,
we left, her at their mercy, there.
A curse which I have borne since then.

ABOUT STEPHEN
Stephen (Cambridge M.A., English & Religious Studies), retired to
Wrexham, Wales from ministry in the Methodist Church due to
Parkinson's Disease. He has had pieces curated by on-line poetry
sites, printed journals and anthologies.
Blog:www.poetrykingsnorth.wordpress.com

Poetry by Martin Willitts Jr.

MATH SAVANT

Incredible — I can "see" equations in my head.
I'm not certain if they've invented the right words for me.
As a child, I stood out, scribbling in notebooks
the four exponentials conjecture on the transcendence
of at least one of four exponential combinations of irrationals.
By now, you are asking, what did he say? I say answers
float in front of me like colors or musical notations.

For years, I could not find the right diagnosis
in the *Diagnostic and Statistical Manual of Mental Disorders*.
Finally, I find a category for me —
apparently, the ability to see numbers as colors is *Synesthesia*,
and as music is *Chromaesthesia*.

In fourth grade, I wrote trigonometry
seeing blue quarter notes in the key of A seventh.
The teacher slapped my hand. She wanted me to focus
on fractions, so I calculated the exact number of students
who would fail the exam. I could explain Brownian Motion
as the random motion of particles suspended in gas.

I drew periodic tables in sixth grade,
wanting to play with chemicals with a mad scientist gleam.
I already understood torque and lift off calculations
before the first rocket went into space. Numbers bored me.

In the Principal's Office, I was instructed to stop
embarrassing the teachers, to normalize, to pretend
numbers were not in a conga line dancing.
They wanted me to "break the solution down,"
but answers were yellow, flashing by my head.
I knew Fermat's Last Theorem
contains a length of 5,320 letters. I can't explain
my unexplainable process;
answers just appear in my head.

ABOUT THE POEM
"The schools did not know what to do with me, and they tried to restrict my math abilities, often accusing me of cheating. I could not do math formulas the "normal way." They stopped letting me take

math courses, and school made me think that something was wrong with me. Kids in school teased me because I was kept out of certain classes. Math was too easy for me. In college, I did all the statistical analysis for the college professors, and then I discovered the 'Diagnostic and Statistical Manual of Mental Disorders'. Finally, I had an explanation for what I was doing and how I did it. But I was treated as if I was 'abnormal,' and some kind of mental illness when I could not 'break down numbers.' This diagnosis places me on the Autism Spectrum. "

ABOUT MARTIN
Martin is a retired Librarian living in Syracuse, New York. He was nominated for 17 Pushcart and 13 Best of the Net awards. Winner of the 2012 Big River Poetry Review's William K. Hathaway Award; 2013 Bill Holm Witness Poetry Contest; 2013 "Trees" Poetry Contest; 2014 Broadsided award; 2014 Dylan Thomas International Poetry Contest; Rattle Ekphrastic Challenge, June 2015, Editor's Choice; Rattle Ekphrastic Challenge, Artist's Choice, November 2016, Stephen A. DiBiase Poetry Prize, 2018; Editor's Choice, Rattle Ekphrastic Challenge, December, 2020; 17th Annual Sejong Writing Competition, 2022. His 21 full-length collections include the Blue Light Award 2019, *The Temporary World*. His recent books are *Harvest Time* (Deerbrook Editions, 2021); *All Wars Are the Same War* (FutureCycle Press, 2022); *Not Only the Extraordinary are Exiting the Dream World* (Flowstone Press, 2022); *Ethereal Flowers* (Shanti Press, 2023); and *Rain Followed Me Home* (Glass Lyre Press, 2023). FB: @martin.j.willitts

Poetry by Til Kumari Sharma

WORDS TO MAKE BUILDING OF MIND

The huge and joyful building of art
Establishes artist with honour.
The respect in literary union
Makes my mind fresh and creative.
The words do not give way to think negatively
Making huge building of art with joy.
To keep tensions in corner
Throwing the mental disorder beside
Brings the home of words
To spend time with fresh creation.

ABOUT TIL
Til is from Parbat, West Nepal. She has published poems, essays, stories and other literary writing in national and international magazines, groups and anthologies.
FB: @Til Kumari Sharma
Blog: www.tilaism-pushpaism.blogspot.com

Peter W. Morris's story

TRAPPED FOR A NIGHT

I sliced my wrists, superficial wounds not meant to kill but to bear evidence of anxiety at a pending divorce. Heading back to work at one of Virginia's most prestigious daily newspapers, my editor-in-chief stopped me upon entrance. "Peter, let me see your wrists." My wife had phoned ahead to notify my employer.

Sleeves of my white Oxford shirt rolled-up, light bloody scratches appeared. "We want to help you," Frank continued. "Ken in sports had a similar problem, so we sent him to a mental health facility for a few nights. It helped. That was five years ago; he's still with us."

Hours later, I entered the doors of the hospital, confident in believing I could leave at any time, as I had been told.

Upon being greeted and shown to my room, I was immediately relieved of my belt, shoes, watch and various toiletries, including a razor, nail file and clippers.

The windows in the single-bed room seemed to flutter, as if some substance covered the glass. "Crazy," I thought. "They think I'm crazy; no, I'm certainly not crazy!"

Flowers began arriving, from my employer, from my friends, from the woman who was at the center of my separation from my wife and two children.

In the middle of my first night, at 3am, an old woman appeared at my bedside. It was creepy in a horror movie scene sort of way; I couldn't understand whatever it was she was babbling, so I turned over and sought renewed sleep.

Come morning and into the afternoon, group classes were dictated, words directed to the day-to-day stresses of life in general. Mostly older residents sat in an 8-10 person circle, some half "out of it" while others feigned interest.

By 3pm, I'd had enough. "I want out of here," I informed the nurse, who notified the administrator. More words of a counseling nature were spoken; with release set, I packed my few belongings, gave away my flowers to others who'd appreciate them more, and headed for the elevator.

Leaning against a tree in front of the hospital, awaiting pickup by "the lady in question," everything seemed settled.

Then two men dressed in white outfits appeared at the door. "We need you to come back to sign a few papers." Willingly, I went back into mental health, where I was met by the administrator, who opened the door to her office.

Suddenly, reality hit. Two men, big men, sent to "get me."

"Peter, I called you back because you gave away your flowers," she explained. "That's a sign of potential self-harm … of suicide."

"WHAT!" I minced no words. "What idiot wrote that directive! Yes, you must think I'm crazy!" A pointless explanation detailed the theory.

Beginning to panic, I fell back of my power over the English language, in which I'd honed my skills as a journalist and writer of numerous books. "I need a VERY convincing argument!" I thought to myself.

"Listen, I love flowers as much as the next man, but I've just lost my home and family, and I'm not sure of where I'll spend the next few nights. Given these facts, why wouldn't I give my flowers to the people who'll still be here after I leave. Simply, I was just trying to bless others confined here with a bit of happiness."

Convinced of sincerity, I was released again. By leaving the mental health facility without employer-mandated healing, my position at the newspaper was terminated.

I was taken to my car, started the engine and drove many miles and many hours to North Carolina, never to return to the site of my downfall. I began a new life, found faith in Jesus Christ and began a newer, healthier relationship with my children.

To this day, I've always been reluctant to inform other people of my one-night incarceration in a mental facility. The stigma of wariness remains within society.

Poetry by Tadala Nkanaunena

... IT HUMBLED ME

I thought I was invincible
that nothing could crumble me
I laughed when one of us got hit with depression
thought he was weak, he was not a man
how wrong I was as it came for me next
slew me in my sleep and woke me to its lair
I could not recognize my own body as it moved lifelessly
day and night, I pretended
smiled and laughed with the rest yet inside I was dying
my best friend became NF as I spiralled deep inside
the four walls of my room became my escape room
they understood my pain and the midnight sighs
they understood my need for solitude, they let me be
it was then that I knew I was like you
I felt how you felt and I did not like it
I thought I was invincible
but ...

ABOUT THE POEM
"The piece was written in remembrance of the time when depression hit me. I could not function as I used to, as life blurred before me. But it taught me that even the strongest still face depression."

ABOUT TADALA
Tadala is an award-winning poet and editor who works with the International Africans Writers Association. Currently residing in Malawi, Tadala is pursuing a Bachelor of Science degree in Computer Science.
FB: @Tadala Nkanaunena

Poetry by Arianna Randall

THE RAIN TELLS US THE TRUTH

Rain brushes my face with soft kisses. lovely
cold and gentle.
all my dreams are of being held
and the nightmares are when I can't save you. my mother said
you need to be gentler with yourself
to prolong your stay in this world.
I think she knew. I'd die simply in a revolution
no grand cause. something small.
for a child, maybe — quietly, alone, with the sun on my face.
and I lived every day like a war.
rain caresses my skin, and the green earth embraces my sadness.
I love windows. stained glass puzzles
as though you can love in pierced pieces of a painful glory. and still
be whole. still be light.
I do not quite know how to be loved.
it is unsettling. the war has taken much
but the rain washes me clean
and I am determined to live.

MORNINGS AND MORNINGS AND MORNINGS

Don't get bitter, get better –
At what? I was always
Too good at survival. Too good at catching breaths
Like lost opportunities. Flower, symbol, sadness, and a
Misbegotten hope for eternity.
Tell me, friend: who told you about pain
Or did it brand your face like a lunar eclipse?
Did it take you? And have you –
Followed it willingly, slipping down the path, fingers clutching
at the dark cloak of escape, pleading to be kept by something.
Who told you that was its name? Pain was an escape, but never
oblivion.
Who told us that light was never weighty, and chains could not be
broken?
What liars!
As though somehow we feel pain
Deeper than anything, knives or oceans or careful secrets.
As though the end erases all beginnings
(and when was pain ever the beginning, anyway? What a

Shoddy story. The universe began in light
It will end that way, too.)
Dear love – pain was a clever cloak of an underneath
Dear hope – the darkness was another lie. A blinding. A stolen kiss
Holding you in a broken embrace.
Dear friend – *it never loved you truly*
But still the light. Still the hope, the grace, the power
Of an unquenched smile. *You were never weak*
Only desperate, and when was desperation a sin?
Another morning, and the brand still burns.
Another morning, and my hands are still heavy.
Another morning, and the waves still tug at my feet
But I never wanted survival; I craved life.
And only one lover could give me that.

JULY 1ST

It is July
and the soft pain of a new month.
it is July
and I float in the water of a boundless ocean to remember there are
things bigger than my fears.
it is July
and I endured every night of the dead month. I shall do it again.
It is July and I have thought of bravery too long.
It is July and after all
it is just another day that slips silently away and leaves me standing.
Another breath, a beat of a heart that
wakes every morning to stare in the mirror.
it is July. and to live is the grandest thing I can do.

ABOUT THE POEMS
*"Poetry, for me, is a constant reminder, not that there is beauty in
the mundane, but that the mundane has always been beautiful; we
are beautiful with our broken pieces and sharp edges; we are beloved
even with the dark corners we are still trying to reconcile ourselves
to. I hope my poems are reminders of the bravery of fighting invisible
battles, and the hopeful truth of every sunrise."*

ABOUT ARIANNA
Arianna is a poet, writer, and star-gazer. She uses poetry as her
greatest coping tool for anxiety, OCD, and depression. She enjoys
hugging trees and cats, reading anything she can get her hands on,
watching the sunrise, and working on her latest novel.

Poetry by Kirk Lawrence-Howard

MOM'S THUMB

I held my mother's hand as
She passed on to whatever
Is next. This is not unknown.

What was forgotten, after,
At the funeral home, all
Arrangements having been made
Long ago, every detail
Signed and sealed and delivered.
In the daze of the son left
Living, small details were lost.
So when the package arrived
Near Christmas, he thought husband
Had ordered a gift for him.
To not ruin the surprise
The package was set aside.
No, husband had no idea;
Didn't recognize the name
Of the sender. A mystery.
A package of the unknown.
Open it. See what it is.

There are small moments in life
That rock the solid foundations
Of your soul. Steal you of breath.
A thumbprint. A small metal
Oval, a memorial
Gift. A tiny remembrance.
Gift from the funeral home,
A print of my late mother's
Right opposable digit.
Incredibly odd, I thought
Like my sweet dead cat's paw print
That I keep in the cupboard.
Hang it from your car mirror
My husband had suggested.
No. Yes. No. Ok, I will.
Now when I am in the car
And my mood is low, or I
Feel alone, I touch my thumb

To hers, and I feel her hand
In mine, feel her close to me.
And now, that odd little gift
Doesn't seem quite so odd
at all.

ABOUT THE POEM
"A remembrance of my mother, and how a small kindness can mean the world."

ABOUT KIRK
Kirk is an actor and voiceover artist who fell in love with poetry and its magical abilities to heal and motivate during Covid. He's now three years into a near-daily project bringing poetry of all types to the world via his YouTube channel.
YouTube: @BespokeVocals

Sonali Sharma's story

THE DUBIOUS DECISION

I realized at the age of 25 that some things that didn't seem right during my childhood days were actually the outcome of a mental illness. An illness persisted inside my house for all these years. The victim was my mother.

As far as I can recall, I always saw her this way. She was careless, angry, and afraid. I thought it was due to her mediocre education, her old-fashioned upbringing, or maybe her basic temperament. I never bothered much as a young, ignorant human being. I remained occupied in my world. I was not aware!

There are a series of odd incidents that now make sense. After the consultation, as I read more about schizophrenia on the Internet, I was able to relate it to those happenings.

Accidents, they say, are very common for a person affected by this mental illness. My mother's obsession with throwing water on the floor is an everyday story. As soon as I wake up in the morning, I see the cemented floor absolutely covered with water. She promises now and then to leave her habit and her obsession, but there has been no improvement as of now. She would stop for a day and tell me she had left her favourite hobby. But soon the reverse would happen. Once, she left a candle on the refrigerator's top, which caught fire. She was busy outside throwing water on the mud, and when she came back, she yelled aloud. Her voice awakened us. We had to use some measures to calm down the fire.

She sits idle every day on a chair and looks outside. She has turned dark. Her vitiligo situation seems to be unstable. She misses her medicines, which she has been taking since she was a little girl. She becomes aggressive very often and blames everyone in the family. She appears too hurtful at times.

As a young girl, I could not form a strong bond with her. As soon as I would say something, she would lash out. She couldn't relate to the emotional bonding between a mother and a child. Of course, patriarchal thinking prevailing in our society could be a major reason for being ignorant about understanding daughters, but in my case, there seemed to be an additional hidden factor. You don't find spiders in your school tiffin because of patriarchy. It is because of a thought state that my mother would be lost in. So, when I was in fourth grade, she probably packed the food without paying attention to the webs and spiders that were relaxing inside the tiffin box.

She had a bad marriage! My father was an alcoholic. She fell in love with him at a young age. Their age difference is vast. Only after a few days of marriage did she realise her wrong decision. She was advised to leave him as soon as she could. But it is not always easy in our world. At that time, remarriage was not seen as a good idea. They said it reflected badly on a woman's loyalty and character. Conventions played their own roles. We have certain stereotypical attitudes towards women, towards their decisions, towards mental illnesses ... towards anything.

She stayed in the same marriage. I was the firstborn child. She slapped me the day she held me in her arms for the first time. How would I get money to marry her off? What will her future be? But I survived and received a good education in a private convent. The money was paid by my mother's brother.

I am a witness to a lot of fights that continue in the house. They have existed ever since I became conscious. Disbelief, noise, ghosts, someone about to do something wrong, worship, and gods are half of the reasons behind these arguments. I told her these things are not realities. There are better things to keep yourself busy with. But it is not as easy as I said.

When suspicion and battles take place in relationships, the bonds can never be soothing. Children born into families where there are constant fights between parents have a very different outlook on relationships. This is altogether a different case, which I will be able to tell more clearly after some years.

Quite some time back, I learned about my mother's mental condition. The doctor told me, *"It is a very tough journey. You need patience and acceptance. Perhaps you never realised this as a child, but now as an adult, you will have to face it. It is painful, I know, and maybe unbelievable as to why it happened with someone you know. Why did God choose your dear one among those 24 million people who actually suffer from this ailment? I know the probability is close to just one person in 300. It may now seem like a rare injustice to you, but life is not always what we expect. It is the bitter truth!"*

We booked a consultation when things got worse. We could see the anger in her eyes. I had just completed my postgraduate studies and came home. For the first time, I heard about symptoms of schizophrenia when I told someone about the situation with my mother. I said she believes in gods and ghosts. I was advised to see a mental health consultant. While booking an appointment, I told her she had always been like this. She is unhappy about her marriage and fears her in-laws will harm her. I once saw her murmuring at night in the small temple inside our house. She is afraid to cross a road. She is fighting with her children. The fights have become worse.

On the visit to the psychologist, she confirmed her condition as schizophrenia. She asked us to keep an eye on her and let her do her usual day-to-day work. There is no cure for the ailment; it can only be diluted. But as soon as medications are stopped, the condition will reappear. We are afraid to give her those heavy doses of medicine. Instead, we requested some sessions that could solve her current trauma. The psychologist had agreed. We are still dubious about our decision. Some days things are fine, and some days they are not. We are still hanging, like any other family where a member is affected by a mental illness.

ABOUT SONALI
Sonali belongs to the hilly state of Uttarakhand in India. She is a postgraduate in environmental studies from Panjab University, Chandigarh. She is an aspiring researcher, a published poet, and a writer. Her poems have appeared in various anthologies and online platforms. She also expresses her views on environmental concerns in *Down to Earth* and *Indian Policy Review*. Apart from her writing and research interests, she has been actively engaged with grassroots organizations working for minority needs.
FB: @Sonali Sharma
Linkedin: @sonali-sharma-884b74143
Instagram: @shonali_1309/

Finding Her Why (Jane's story)

By Shannon Hodges, Ph.D.

As a professional counsellor of nearly 40-years, both in academia and in clinical practice, I have witnessed people crumbling under the burden of trauma, mental illness, neglect, and addiction but also seen remarkable recovery from people on the brink of abject destruction. Few patients bring this amazing turnaround to light better than a woman I shall refer to as Jane (pseudonym).

Jane was a thirty-something, single parent, Caucasian female, court remanded for substance abuse treatment. She had lost custody of her two young children after an arrest for drunk driving while her children were passengers in her vehicle. Given previous charges related to substance abuse, Jane was court-mandated for counselling at our rural clinic. Failure to complete treatment would result in termination of all parental rights and incarceration. She sat sullenly in the waiting room, arms tightly crossed staring straight ahead and mute when I introduced myself. At my office I commenced with the informed consent phase preceding treatment. I explained my role in addition to counselling was to author a report to the judge at the conclusion of treatment. That report would determine in part whether she would regain custody of her children. She already knew that completing treatment successfully was a condition for remaining out of jail. Scribbling her signature acknowledging she understood she then turned away from me.

Diagnosed with Alcohol Abuse Disorder and Borderline Personality Disorder, Jane self-medicated her pain and lashed out in anger at perceived threats. I had treated scores of patients like Jane and her angry presentation was common faire. Her silent "Fuck you!" projection was expected, albeit unpleasant animus. Unable to pull words from patients mouths nor simply change their attitude with any magic words, I deferred to my straightforward approach. I opened, "You'd like to be done with counselling, right?" Suddenly, she turned towards me in interest. "You fucking putting me on?" she asked, streetwise wariness evident across her features. I shook my head. "Okay then, just write the judge and tell him I'm good to go." I explained my having previously collaborated with this judge and emphasized he would require specific evidence of her sobriety and attitudinal change including clean urine screens, attending weekly 12-step meetings, and a letter from me stating she had completed treatment and would be a responsible parent. My response triggered her, sending her into a profanity-laced tirade that while impressive in volume, creativity, and duration, was predictable. Patiently waiting until she ceased her roar, I inquired if she would like to regain custody of her kids. Wariness back, she nodded. I explained she would need to help me write this pivotal letter to the judge. Furthermore, should she force me to author the letter in her absence, she would be most unhappy with the result. After a long, sceptical pause, she nodded.

As she had already completed the intake, we moved into regular session. Jane acknowledged having been involved with the mental health system since childhood. She recounted a chaotic childhood with an alcoholic father and constant bickering between her parents with arguments occasionally escalating into physical violence. More than once her mother needed medical care after her father's violent episodes. Her parents eventually divorced, and her mother commenced a string of boyfriends, all of whom abused alcohol and drugs. Custody of Jane and her younger brother eventually transferred to her maternal grandparents who, while stable, were in ill health, impoverished and unable to provide adequate care. Jane began acting out in high school, staying out late, drinking alcohol and becoming sexually active at age 15. Raped by a 20-year-old date was her first sexual experience. Thereafter, she became sexually promiscuous, becoming pregnant at 17 (she had an abortion). Jane admitted she began abusing alcohol and smoking weed regularly, dropped out of school, and married her ex-husband, giving birth to two children. Her spouse-maintained employment yet was alcohol dependent, abusive, and an indifferent parent. She divorced him when the children were in primary school, and he had no further involvement in their kids' lives.

Sadly, Jane's story follows an all-too familiar pattern: a child removed from an abusive home, begins experimenting with alcohol, drugs, and sex, becomes pregnant as a teenager, marries an addicted, abusive man, creating the same type of dysfunctional relationships she grew up with. Psychiatrist Albert Bandura termed this Social Modelling Theory whereby we learn and subsequently repeat behaviours via observation of significant role models (i.e., parents). Jane observed that in family relationships men are violent to women, verbal abuse is common, and alcohol and other drug abuse is commonplace. Thus, Jane's *normal* involved significant abuse and very little affection. Coping supports were not responsible parents, educators, spiritual figures, or therapists, as experience had taught authority figures were untrustworthy. Rather, observing her parents and peers reach for chemical substances to dull their pain, she naturally did the same.

As humanely as possible, I summarized her story inquiring if I had heard correctly and whether she had considered that trauma, and not addiction being the real culprit. For the first time she entertained a question seriously. She had never considered trauma an issue despite experiencing long-term physical, verbal abuse, and a sexually assault. Looking at me straight on she said without guile, "This was just my normal." Sensing a teachable moment, I asked how she would like to raise her children. She became teary and admitted she wanted better for her two children. Inquiring what *better* might look like, she answered better would be a sober mom and no abusive, addicted male partners. "Okay, how might you begin to create that healthy home for you and your kids?" She shook her head, look of genuine puzzlement on her features.

I have counselled scores like Jane who desire a better life for themselves and their offspring but are clueless on how to create it. It should be unsurprising the Jane's of the world who have known significant abuse, neglect, and self-medication from an early age do not know how to solve their problem, given dysfunction constantly modelled for them. Bandura's theory that children grow up to re-enact behaviours modelled during formative childhood has proved powerfully true innumerable times in my protracted career. Yet, a privileged, often clueless society points its accusing finger at the Jane's, unaware of their past, offering no better solution than punishment and scathing moral judgment. As she was an expert in how to fail, my suggestion was that we strategize on how to create a healthy life for herself and her kids. Reluctantly, she agreed.

I have generally found standard talk therapy of limited viability when treating traumatized patients. Research by Francine Shapiro, Bessel van der Kolk, and others suggests a mind-body-breath approach. My clients have danced, sang, read aloud their poetry, meditated, painted, drawn, and acted out scenes from their past, among various interventions. Few could abide sitting through otherwise efficacious approaches like Cognitive Behaviour Therapy (CBT). As Jane had offered colouring and drawing being hobbies she enjoyed, the following session I brought in posters, crayons, and coloured pencils and instructed her to draw the life she would like for her and her kids. Momentarily inert, she shrugged and commenced drawing. I sat back and observed her creative opus. Some 30-minutes later she held up her poster for review. I taped it to the whiteboard and asked her to explain it to me. Jane had drawn a picture with bright colours, sunshine, a small home with well-tended flower garden, and three happy people-her and her kids. People on the periphery sporting smiles were her mother and friends. She explained this was the life she wanted to create while admitting there would be rain, occasional tears, and arguments with her children, mother, and friends.

We conjointly processed her drawing. She admitted having never considered a personal vision, nor could recall anyone in her circle doing so. Nearing session's end I assigned her homework. Providing her drawing utensils and poster paper, I requested she draw how she might begin to create the vision she had just drawn. I further cautioned such creation takes time, but emphasized concrete reminders like drawings can be particularly important and encouraging. I further reiterated that continued attendance at 12-step meetings and maintaining sobriety were absolute requirements. Finally, I explained we needed to heal her trauma, otherwise relapse via self-medication with alcohol was likely. Jane nodded, quietly gathered the art supplies, and left; her exit a radical departure from her arrival.

The following session Jane brought in two drawings. In one she drew her AA meeting, with her and others in a circle, talking with her AA sponsor, and refusing alcohol from an old friend. The drawing also illustrated her working at her low-wage convenience store job, and her and her kids in her mother's small, dilapidated home. She stated Family Services had recently approved her living in the home with her mother and kids provided she maintained sobriety and attended therapy with me. The second drawing was future-oriented showing her in class at the local community college ("Psychology class"), her and her kids in a comfortable home, with a well-maintained yard landscaped with bright flowers. "These drawings show how I will create my vision," she offered. I nodded and asked if she were ready to work towards her goal. She nodded, serious look about her face.

We began by focusing her anger, something quite common in trauma survivors. She reported when she felt anxious, she verbally attacked others. She described a building rage that resulted in her "blowing up" at someone, resulting in job insecurity and loss of friends. I explained distress tolerance; meaning we'd need to approach her trauma to heal it. I offered that anytime the treatment was too much, she was to say *"Stop."* We role played her getting triggered verbally and just prior to her blowing up, I coached her in grounding using 5-senses: 5 things you see, 4 you hear, 3 you can smell, 2 you can touch and 1 you can taste (or simpler, clap hands and stomp feet). After several role plays, she made moderate improvement. I assigned her the 5-senses approach whenever she felt herself getting angry and family, friends, or co-workers. I also have her practice 4-square breathing (4 second slow inhale, 4 second slow exhale). Finally, as I was introducing bodywork, she divulged having just joined a yoga class along with her AA sponsor. I encouraged her to continue with yoga as a means of working the trauma out of her body.

Over several sessions we utilized a trauma treatment workbook to address faulty cognitions ("I'm a loser," "hopeless parent," "sobriety impossible," etc.), somatic issues, and breath work. Fortunately, buoyed by her recent promotion to assistant manager at work, her mood improved. Once again, I assigned her homework to draw how she was healing from trauma. The following session she brought in an impressive drawing highlighting healing in her mind, body, and breath with her in yoga class, meditating before bed, and in our counselling sessions. She drew a second picture of how treatment was improving her relationship with her kids, mother, and friends. Fearing things sounded too good, I inquired about any regression. She admitted to a couple of disagreements at work, but emphasized having managed them better than previously. Inquiring on a healing scale of 1 to 10, with higher better, she rated her weekly success of anxiety management at 6 or 7. She reiterated her AA sponsor, 12-step meetings and our therapy sessions as being immensely helpful in her success.

As Jane maintained sobriety and we focused on trauma-focused therapy, she continued with slight but steady improvements. She did become triggered during sessions - something common in trauma treatment given the need to address emotional triggers - and periodically her ingrained behaviour of lashing out in verbal abuse occurred. With each outburst, we focused on her 5-senses, 4-square breathing, and then either redid the intervention or if she were unable to proceed, she would just say, "Not now," or "I need to take a break," meaning she would stand and walk about my office until settled. Then we would either continue with the line of treatment, or move to a less invasive intervention. Her touchstone however was her drawings and our subsequent discussions of them. One of her more interesting drawings involved drawing her healing. She drew and described the three phases of mind-body-breath healing, working on replacing negative thoughts 5-times per day, doing body positions in yoga class, and her 5-senses grounding within and outside session. While acknowledging all components of treatment were helpful, she emphasized her drawing was the most important helpful. Inquiring why, she stated, "It reminds me of what's possible in life. Previously I never considered having a choice."

We continued with a mind-body-breath approach, augmented with her drawings, and after 15 weeks Jane successfully completed treatment. Unsurprisingly, she did have a brief relapse when getting together with an old friend, however, after a couple of drinks, she left the bar and called her sponsor: "I blew nearly four months sobriety," she sighed in teary-eyed disappointment. I counselled her to apply self-compassion having not gone 4-months without substance abuse since her mid-teens (she was mid-30s) and to focus on the *one day at a time* mantra her 12-step program utilized. She acknowledged her former self would not have continued with AA and counselling, even with the threat of jail time and loss of her kids. She also reported her trauma and anxiety scores outside session (the 1 to 10 ratings, 10 being high) were consistently below 5, another encouraging sign. Her AA sponsor informed me Jane had been diligent in attending meetings, and her urine screens were clean - her brief relapse notwithstanding. During our final session, I asked what had been most important in her trauma reduction and sobriety. She cited her sponsor's support, our sessions, and added, "The drawing work was so powerful." To put the period on our sessions, I had her speak to her former self using Psychodrama founder Jacob Moreno's empty chair intervention, something I had prepared her for weeks earlier. Placing an empty chair directly across from her, I asked her to put her previously addicted, traumatized self into the chair and speak with her, encouraging self-compassion. Nodding, she praised her former self for surviving an abusive, chaotic life, sticking with counselling, and attending all AA meetings. I then asked her to switch chairs and play her former speaking to her current self. She complied, and her former self thanked her current self for her perseverance, completing counselling, her promotion at work, and her enrolling for a psychology course at the community college. She shed tears and then with a smile, pulled out a poster drawing with her completing therapy, playing to her children, practicing yoga with her sponsor, and helping her mother with house chores. I congratulated her, we shook hands, and she walked out having completed four intense months of trauma-centred therapy.

Several months later a still sober Jane visited me at the clinic. She was taking one course per term at the community college, and planned to complete an associate degree in business, hoping to eventually complete a baccalaureate degree and move into a better career. Relatives were helping her family make basic renovations to her mom's home, and she now held joint custody of her kids with her mother. She acknowledged occasionally feeling the desire to drink, but always activated her plan of calling her sponsor. She continued with yoga classes, and now managed the convenience store. Recently she had joined a trauma thrivers support group run by a colleague of mine. I praised her for her success and resilience. She chuckled and then withdrew a large colour drawing with a line down the middle. The line separated her previous traumatized, addicted life from that of her current sober, healthier one. The contrast between the two sides was remarkable in colour, affect, and physical representation. "I attend AA meetings religiously, but drawing is what keeps hope and possibility alive," she said.

Philosopher Friedrich Nietzsche wrote a person with a *why* could overcome any *how*. I have long maintained to students, colleagues, and friends that counselling primarily involves helping clients discover their *why*. Jane's *why* lay in the creative process of drawing her vision, motivating her to work those tall, life-long steps of sobriety, become a better parent and start the arduous journey towards a more fulfilling life. Tragically, many like Jane are modelled only how to fail, never comprehending they have choices. Although counsellor and not philosopher, experience suggests understanding the importance of a *why* means being taught potential dangers of the *how*. Like Jane, many are unschooled on the why, but learn all-too well the destruction the various how's can wreak upon their lives. Jane found her why, but I could author many tragic stories of those who never found theirs.

Find your why.

www.PoetryForMentalHealth.org

Made in the USA
Monee, IL
17 September 2023